Four Pillars
and
Oriental Medicine

Four Pillars
and
Oriental Medicine

Celestial Stems, Terrestrial Branches and Five Elements for Health

David Twicken, Ph.D., L.Ac.

Writers Club Press
San Jose New York Lincoln Shanghai

Four Pillars and Oriental Medicine
Celestial Stems, Terrestrial Branches and Five Elements for Health

Writers Club Press
an imprint of iUniverse.com, Inc.

For information address:
iUniverse.com, Inc.
620 North 48th Street, Suite 201
Lincoln, NE 68504-3467
www.iuniverse.com

ISBN: 0-595-1968-4

Printed in the United States of America

Disclaimer

The information in this book is based on the author's knowledge and personal experience. It is presented for educational purposes to assist the reader in expanding their knowledge of Asian philosophy and Oriental Medicine. Before using any of the techniques in this book consult a licensed physician for advice on whether or not to practice these techniques. The techniques and practices are to be used at the reader's own discretion and liability. The author is not responsible in any manner whatsoever for any injury that may occur by following the instructions in this book.

Acknowledgments

I t is with my deepest gratitude I thank Mr. Gary Lam for his assistance in understanding the Chinese Calendar. Special thanks to Susan Morse, M.T.O.M. for her editing and friendship. Thank you Mr. Mantak Chia and the Healing Tao for their illustrations.

Author Contact:
www.ChineseAstrologyNow.com

About this Book

This is the first English publication solely dedicated to the Four Pillars and Oriental Medicine. It is designed to accomplish three major goals. The first goal is to introduce the foundation principles of Asian philosophy in a clear, logical and user-friendly way. These basic principles can be applied to all Asian Arts, including Oriental Medicine, Chinese Astrology and Feng Shui. The second goal is to introduce the Chinese Calendar. This calendar is the key to revealing an ancient, esoteric, universal code that can be applied to all aspects of Four Pillars. I have created a user-friendly English translation of the Chinese Calendar; this will assist in making a complicated calculation quick and easy. Access to this calendar provides a key to opening the door to the deepest aspects of Four Pillars science. The third goal is to apply Four Pillars to Oriental Medicine. The primary focus is using the Four Pillars as a tool to identify the pre-natal or constitutional condition. Secondarily, future cycles of time provide post-natal influences, the combination of pre-natal and post-natal energies influence health throughout a lifetime. Finally, one of the most esoteric and closely guarded Acupuncture methods is introduced, Chronotherapeutics or Time Acupuncture. This ancient system connects cycles of Time, Vital Substances and Acupuncture.

Contents

Introduction

Traditional Oriental Medicine has been practiced for thousands of years, it is a natural healing system which has evolved into a systematic art and science practiced in every continent throughout the world. Acupuncture, Herbal Medicine, Tai Chi Chuan and Qi Gong have become household words in the West. The popularity of these natural healing methods has become so influential traditional western medical communities have incorporated them into their practice. Hospitals and clinics are working with Acupuncturists; physicians are being trained in Oriental Medicine, and most major insurance companies throughout the United States now cover Acupuncture. If we look to the future it is clear the healing modality for the 21st century will be a combination of Eastern and Western modalities.

For the past three decades there has been an explosion in the breadth and depth of Oriental Medical knowledge in the western community. One area that has been kept a closely guarded secret is the connection between one's birthday and health. This method is commonly referred to as the Four Pillars. Four Pillars reflects aspects of the constitutional health condition. Woman and Man are comprised of Universal energies, which include influences from stars, planets, water, plants, mountains and magnetic energies, Figure A and B. This unique birth condition provides a code that reveals the health condition of the internal organs. Four Pillars is an effective tool to identify constitutional health conditions. It also clearly identifies the health influences of future cycles of time or post-natal influences.

Figure A

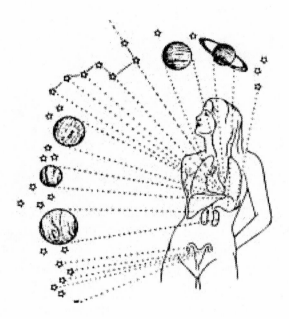

Figure B

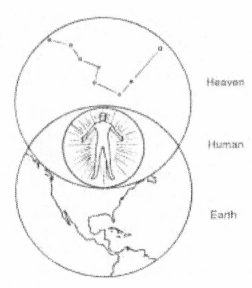

Calculating a birth chart or "Four Pillars" is the initial step in performing a Four Pillars health evaluation. This information is obtained from the ancient 10,000-Year Chinese Calendar. This calendar includes the energetic influence of each Hour, Day, Month and Year. Because the complete Chinese calendar has been largely inaccessible in the West, this system has not been fully revealed to the western community. A *Chinese Calendar* consists of four major parts: Stems, Branches, Five Elements and Solar months. Because this information can be difficult to obtain, I have created an English translation of the Chinese Calendar, "Chinese Calendar Made Easy ©". This calendar is user-friendly, allowing easy access to the deepest levels of Four Pillars for Health. In a short period of time you will be able to construct a Four Pillars birth chart in less than 60 seconds.

Chapter 1

Life Force

The ancient Asian cosmological view is that the Universe is filled with an energy that flows through infinite cycles of transformation. This energy comprises all of life, including stars, planets, trees, mountains, water, animals and human Life. This energy is referred to as Qi. Qi is both energy and matter. It is also the force that allows the transformation from energy to matter and matter to energy. For example, Water is a type of Qi and is a perfect example of how Qi transforms. Water can be in the form of ice; ice can transform into Water and Water into steam. Qi is ice, Qi is Water, Qi is steam and Qi is the heat that allows the transformation to occur. Qi is all of life. Every part of the universe is a blend of different types of Qi. To understand this blending of Qi is to understand life. Knowing the rhythms and expressions of Qi is the basis for predicting and transforming life.

The human body is comprised of Qi. Bones, tendons and muscles are dense forms of Qi. Blood and energy are subtler forms of Qi; spirit is the subtlest form of Qi. Cycles of growth are examples of different ways Qi moves or unfolds. The transformation from infancy to childhood, childhood to adolescence and adolescence to adulthood is slow and gradual. This process reflects one way Qi unfolds. Another process can be explained by exercising muscles. Exercising muscles causes quick changes in strength and shape. Natural transformations can not be altered to make an infant become a child faster. The inherit unfolding of this Qi process is very different than the quick development of exercising muscles. Some forms of Qi are slow, others are fast, and knowing the influences of Qi is the foundation for developing an effective system to manage Qi and

1

health. A Four Pillars health condition is a Qi condition, it reflects constitutional health. This knowledge reveals excesses and deficiencies in organ systems. Acupuncture, Herbs, Bodywork, Qi Gong, Foods and Feng Shui are techniques to affect a person's Qi. Qi can be tonified, sedated or harmonized to obtain vitality and optimal health.

All tools used in Four Pillars and Oriental Medicine are variations of Qi. This book introduces Yin-Yang, Five Elements, Stems, Branches and cycles of time, which are all different aspects or transformations of Qi. These tools help calculate the effects of Qi throughout a lifetime. Knowing how Qi works, which includes how it is affected by foods, exercise, mental outlook, emotions and cycles of time is the essence of the art and science of Four Pillars and Oriental Medicine.

Chapter 2

Yin-Yang

From the beginning of time, humans have searched to understand Heaven, Earth and Human life, whether it was Hindus in India, Aztecs in Mexico, Jews of Israel or ancient Egyptians. In China, a model of understanding nature evolved which would become the root of Chinese philosophy, Medicine, Nutrition, Martial Arts, Feng Shui and Astrology. This system is Yin-Yang. Yin-Yang theory includes viewing the Universe as one integrated whole, as well as two opposing, but interdependent elements. All aspects of life can be categorized into Yin-Yang. For example, Heaven-Earth, Man-Woman, Hot-Cold, Left-Right, Light-Dark, Front-Back, Hard-Soft, North-South, East-West, Root-Branch, Top-Bottom and Fast-Slow are two sides of one phenomenon. Yin-Yang theory categories any situation into two parts; each part gives life to its opposite. There must be a Left to have a Right, a Strong to have a Weak, a Front to have a Back. They are not two separate entities; they are two sides of the same situation.

Yin-Yang is a predominant component in Four Pillars. One major application of Yin-Yang theory is that Yang represents a growing or expanding phase, and Yin, a declining phase. All of life flows through this basic model of waxing and waning. Each expansion leads to a decline, which leads to another expansion and another decline in an endless cycle. In Four Pillars the first step is determining the condition of each element and the second step is to relate that condition to the internal organs and Acupuncture channels. Each organ-channel will be Yang-excess, Yin-deficient or balanced. If a disease is acute it is considered Yang, if a disease is chronic it is Yin. When a disease is caused by lifestyle it is Yang, when it is caused by a constitutional condition, it is Yin. Yin-Yang permeates every aspect of Four Pillars for health.

Chapter 3

Five Elements

The Five Elements are the basis or foundation of the Four Pillars. They are the ABC's of calculating, evaluating and applying knowledge of the Four Pillars. The following explains the Five Elements.

This circle is an integrated whole. It represents the oneness of life.

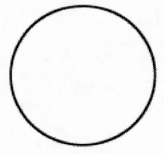

A circle can also be viewed as two parts, the top is Yang and the bottom is Yin.

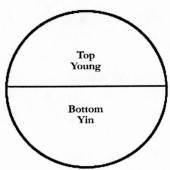

This same circle can be viewed with five phases, the Five Elements.

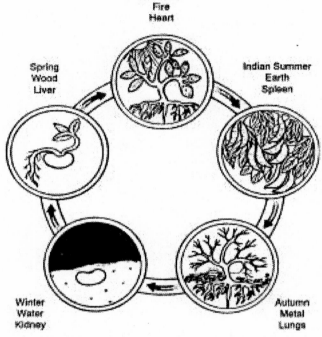

Each segment is assigned an element: Water, Wood, Fire, Earth and Metal. Each element maintains a position within the circle. For example, Wood is positioned where the circle begins to move upward and represents growth or Springtime; Fire is located where the portion of the circle reaches its peak, symbolizing Summer; Earth is positioned where harvesting takes place, representing Indian Summer; Metal represents turning inward or contraction, representing Autumn, and Water is where the circle turns completely inward to regenerate, representing Winter. Water also portrays preparation for a new Spring, Wood or growth cycle. This cycle continues infinitely and reflects self-generation and the eternal nature of life.

The relative position of each of the Five Elements or Five Phases in the circle determines its specific relationship with every other element. For example, Water is the mother to Wood, grandparent to Fire, grandchild of Earth and child of Metal. Each element has those distinct relationships with the four remaining elements. The ability to apply those relationships is crucial to Four Pillars for health. Table 3a summarizes these relationships.

Table 3a

Element ——▶	Water	Wood	Fire	Earth	Metal
Parent	Metal	Water	Wood	Fire	Earth
Sibling—Same	Water	Wood	Fire	Earth	Metal
Child – Offspring	Wood	Fire	Earth	Metal	Water
Grandchild	Fire	Earth	Metal	Water	Wood
Grandparent Controller	Earth	Metal	Water	Wood	Fire

Interpreting this chart.

Water's parent is Metal.
Water's sibling is Water.
Water's child is Wood.
Water's grandchild is Fire.
Water's Controller is Earth.

From these five relationships we see five key interactions.

1. Each element gives to another element. The parent.
2. Each element controls another element. The grandparent or controller.
3. Each element is controlled by another element. The grandchild.
4. Each element receives from another element. The child.
5. Each element is supported by another element. The same or sibling.

These relationships are expressed in the actions of giving, receiving, controlling and being controlled. Obtaining a natural healthy life depends on finding balance within these five interactions. One action is not better than another, there is only meaning when a situation is compared to a particular birth chart. Some people need to be nourished, others need control, and still others need to give. What is beneficial is relative to the condition of all elements in the Four Pillars. Each of the relationships can be balanced, excessive, or deficient. Four Pillars is a tool that reveals how the Universe created a Five Elements combination at birth. Upon evaluating the strengths and weaknesses of a birth chart, one can calculate how Five Element cycles of time affect a person. Predicting influences on health are based on Hourly, Daly, Monthly and Yearly energy cycles.

Table 3b

Situation	First Action	Second Action
Weakness	Nourish. Add the Parent Element. Add same – Sibling element.	Add a small amount of the Grandparent element to make the Parent stronger when appropriate.
Too Strong or Excessive	Control. Add the Grandparent.	Reduce. Add the Child element to drain the overly strong parent.

The following diagrams illustrate how each element is affected by all elements. Determine which elements are needed when an excessive or weakness exists. Confirm your choices with Table 3c below.

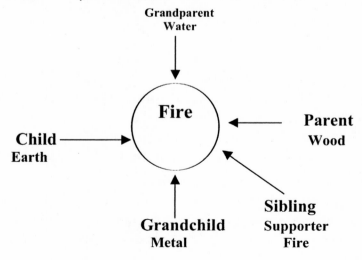

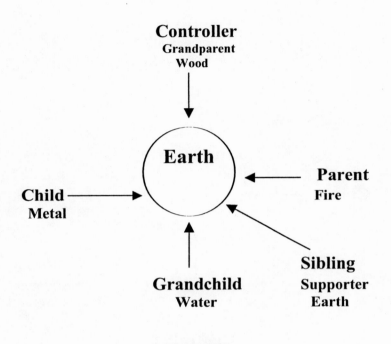

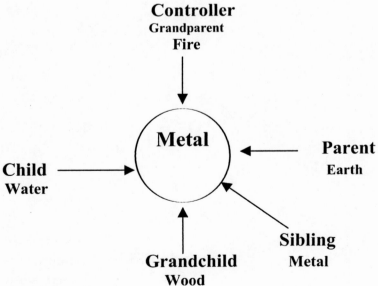

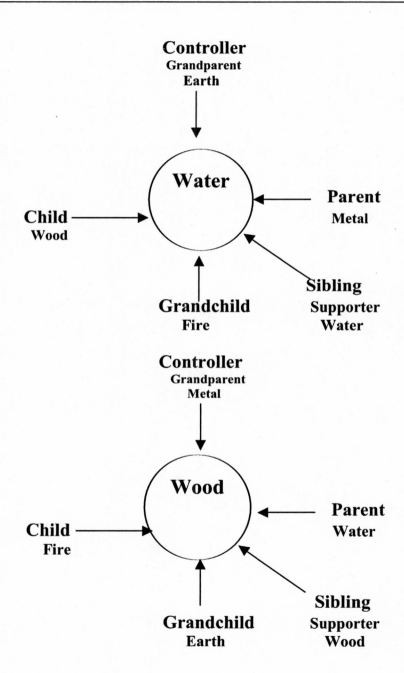

Table 3c

Element	Corrections for Excess	Corrections for Weakness
Water	Earth, Wood	Metal, Water
Wood	Metal, Fire	Water, Wood
Fire	Water, Earth	Wood, Fire
Earth	Wood, Metal	Fire, Earth
Metal	Fire, Water	Earth, Metal

The Five Elements interact in a variety of ways. The major cycles are the promotion, controlling and sedation cycles. These three cycles provide the basis for most applications of Four Pillars for Health. The illustrations below explain each cycle.

Promotion Cycle

The Promotion cycle is the Parent to Child relationship within the Five Elements. It is a cycle that nourishes, supplements or strengthens the child element. Its influence can be favorable or unfavorable; it depends on the condition of the elements. The following diagram illustrates the Promotion cycle.

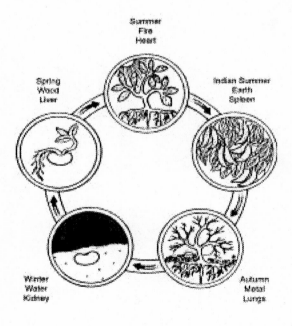

Promotion Cycle

1. If Water is placed on Wood, it will grow. Water is the mother of Wood.
2. If Wood is placed in a Fire, the Fire will grow. Wood is the mother of Fire.
3. Fire will turn substances into Ashes or Earth. Fire is the Mother of Earth.
4. Metal is found within Earth. Earth is the Mother of Metal.
5. Metal can be liquefied into Water. Metal is the Mother of Water.

Controlling Cycle

The controlling cycle is the grandparent to grandchild relationship. Its influence can be favorable or unfavorable, it depends on the conditions of the elements. The following diagram illustrates the controlling cycle.

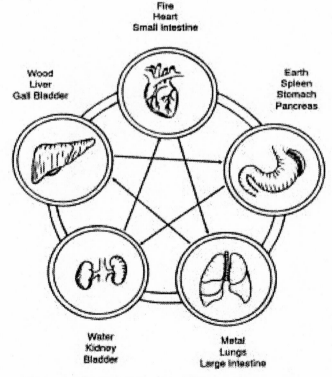

The arrows direct the controlling cycle sequence.

Controlling Cycle

1. Fire melts Metal or controls Metal. Grandparent relationship.
2. Metal cuts Wood or controls Wood. Grandparent relationship.
3. Wood absorbs nutrients from the Earth and controls Earth. Grandparent relationship.
4. Earth absorbs Water or controls Water. Grandparent relationship.
5. Water puts out Fire or controls Fire. Grandparent relationship.

Sedation Cycle

T he Controlling cycle either controls, dominates or weakens. When the controlling cycle is overactive and creates an imbalance, the Sedation cycle is used to correct the Controlling cycle. In most cases, the Controlling cycle creates unfavorable Health conditions and needs to be corrected. The Promotion and Sedation cycles are arranged identically, the only difference is the flow of energy. The Promotional cycle flows clockwise and the Sedation cycle flows counter-clockwise. All three cycles are used in Chinese Astrology, Feng Shui and Four Pillars and Oriental Medicine.

Sedation Cycle

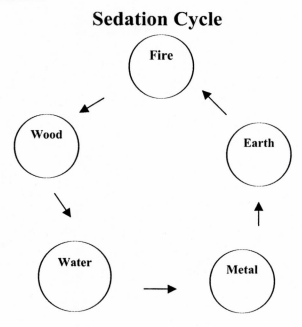

Sedation Cycle

1. Water is the child of Metal. Water takes from Metal, reducing its influence.
2. Metal is the child of Earth. Metal takes from Earth, reducing its influence.
3. Earth is the child of Fire. Earth takes from Fire, reducing its influence.
4. Fire is the child of Wood. Fire takes from Wood, reducing its influence.
5. Wood is the child of Water. Wood takes from Water, reducing its influence.

Chapter 4

Energy Cycles

The Four Pillars is a marvelous illustration of our relationship to nature. It is a systematic method of calculating nature's influences. The Application of Yin-Yang, Five Elements and cycles of time provides the vehicle for calculating a birth chart that reflects the natal or constitutional condition. This birth chart is called the Four Pillars and is based on the influences of time, particularly Hours, Days, Months and Years. As with all of life, time can be categorized into Yin-Yang, Yang is a Heavenly Stem and Yin is an Earthly Branch.

Cycles of time are also categorized into the Five Elements: Water, Wood, Fire, Earth and Metal. Each element contains a Yin and Yang aspect, for example, the 10 Heavenly Stems are Yang Wood, Yin Wood, Yang Fire, Yin Fire, Yang Earth, Yin Earth, Yang Metal, Yin Metal, Yang Water, Yin Water. The 12 Earthly Branches include the Five Elements with their Yin-Yang quality, totaling 10 Branches. They also have an additional Earth branch that contains a Yin and Yang aspect, producing 12 Branches. Earth is a transformer; it transforms one element or season into another. That is why there are two extra Earth elements, one Yin and one Yang. (This will be explained throughout the book). The 12 Branches are Yang Wood, Yin Wood, Yang Earth, Yang Fire, Yin Fire, Yin Earth, Yang Metal, Yin Metal, Yang Earth, Yin Water Yang Water, Yin Earth. Notice the Earthly Branches are between changes from one element to another. Branches can also be referred to by their Chinese Zodiac Animal name. (See Table 4a).

Stems and Branches represent a flow of energy; each Hour, Day, Month and Year is made up of one combination of a Stem and Branch. Each specific Stem and Branch combination is called a Binomial. Binomials are organized in a cycle of 60, which includes every combination of Stems and Branches. Six cycles of 10 Stems and five cycles of 12 Branches equals one cycle of 60. Hours, Days, Months and Years contain those Stem and Branch energy combinations. *Table 4a contains the 60 binomial cycle.* A birth chart has four Binomials, one Binomial for the Hour, Day, Month and Year. Those four units of time create the birth chart or the Four Pillars. The Four Pillars are the foundation for Classical Five Element Chinese Astrology and are also applied to health. In Table 4a, binomial one includes Yang Wood, number two has Yin Wood and the Five Elements continue until Binomial 10. Yang Wood reappears again at 11, 21, 31, 41 and 51. The 10 Stems continue for six cycles, completing a cycle of 60. The Branch Rat, begins at number 1 and the 12 Animals or Branches continue until they repeat again with the Rat, at 13, 25, 37 and 49.

Table 4a

Stem and Branch Cycle of 60

For Hours, Days, Months and Years

Number	1	2	3	4	5	6
Stem	Yang Wood	Yin Wood	Yang Fire	Yin Fire	Yang Earth	Yin Earth
Branch	Rat	Ox	Tiger	Rabbit	Dragon	Snake
Number	7	8	9	10	11	12
Stem	Yang Metal	Yin Metal	Yang Water	Yin Water	Yang Wood	Yin Wood
Branch	Horse	Sheep	Monkey	Cock	Dog	Pig
Number	13	14	15	16	17	18
Stem	Yang Fire	Yin Fire	Yang Earth	Yin Earth	Yang Metal	Yin Metal
Branch	Rat	Ox	Tiger	Rabbit	Dragon	Snake
Number	19	20	21	22	23	24
Stem	Yang Water	Yin Water	Yang Wood	Yin Wood	Yang Fire	Yin Fire
Branch	Horse	Sheep	Monkey	Cock	Dog	Pig
Number	25	26	27	28	29	30
Stem	Yang Earth	Yin Earth	Yang Metal	Yin Metal	Yang Water	Yin Water
Branch	Rat	Ox	Tiger	Rabbit	Dragon	Snake
Number	31	32	33	34	35	36
Stem	Yang Wood	Yin Wood	Yang Fire	Yin Fire	Yang Earth	Yin Earth
Branch	Horse	Sheep	Monkey	Cock	Dog	Pig
Number	37	38	39	40	41	42
Stem	Yang Metal	Yin Metal	Yang Water	Yin Water	Yang Wood	Yin Wood
Branch	Rat	Ox	Tiger	Rabbit	Dragon	Snake
Number	43	44	45	46	47	48
Stem	Yang Fire	Yin Fire	Yang Earth	Yin Earth	Yang Metal	Yin Metal
Branch	Horse	Sheep	Monkey	Cock	Dog	Pig
Number	49	50	51	52	53	54
Stem	Yang Water	Yin Water	Yang Wood	Yin Wood	Yang Fire	Yin Fire
Branch	Rat	Ox	Tiger	Rabbit	Dragon	Snake
Number	55	56	57	58	59	60
Stem	Yang Earth	Yin Earth	Yang Metal	Yin Metal	Yang Water	Yin Water
Branch	Horse	Sheep	Monkey	Cock	Dog	Pig

Branch	Pig	Rat	Ox	Tiger	Rabbit	Dragon	Snake	Horse	Sheep	Monkey	Cock	Dog
Main Element	Yang Water	Yin Water	Yin Earth	Yang Wood	Yin Wood	Yang Earth	Yang Fire	Yin Fire	Yin Earth	Yang Metal	Yin Metal	Yang Earth

The box above reflects the main element for each of the Branches or animals. They reflect the inner-method for determining Branch-Animal polarity. This is explained in Chapter 5.

Heavenly Stems are in the top row and represent Heavenly or Yang influences. They are always named as a Five Element: for example, Yang Wood, Yin Wood, Yang Fire or Yin Fire. The lower row contains Earthly Branches or Chinese Zodiac Animals. They can be named as a Five Element or as an Animal. I recommend using the Animal name because it helps differentiate Branches from Stems, and Branches from Branches, especially since there are four Earthly Branches. Either system can be utilized. The 60 Binomials include every possible energy combination; each Hour, Day, Month and Year has a Binomial.

The diagram below shows the Four Pillars, it is the foundation for a Four Pillars analysis. Stems and Branches are found in the Chinese Calendar and placed in the Hour, Day, Month and Year Pillars or Palaces.

Four Pillars

Hour	Day	Month	Year
Stem	Stem	Stem	Stem
Branch Animal	Branch Animal	Branch Animal	Branch Animal

Chapter 5

Branches or Chinese Zodiac Animals

D iagram 5a illustrates the 12 Terrestrial or Earthly Branches and their corresponding main element, Chinese zodiac Animal, geographical location and position. This diagram assists in understanding many of the interactions of two or more Branches.

Branches or Animals in the same geographical area have an affinity for each other. They share the same element and therefore support or reinforce each other. In addition, a Trinity or Harmonic relation between each fourth Animal creates a positive relationship. For example, Cock, Ox and Snake are four places apart from each other and therefore are compatible. This dynamic is very important and is explained in the chapter on Branch combinations. The cardinal or middle positions also have a special relationship with their opposite cardinal position. The Cock and Rabbit, and Rat and Horse, oppose each other creating a spark, causing excitement, pressure and stress. Branches exert favorable or unfavorable influences on other Stems and Branches, the influence depends on the condition of each element. This process is explained throughout the book.

Diagram 5a

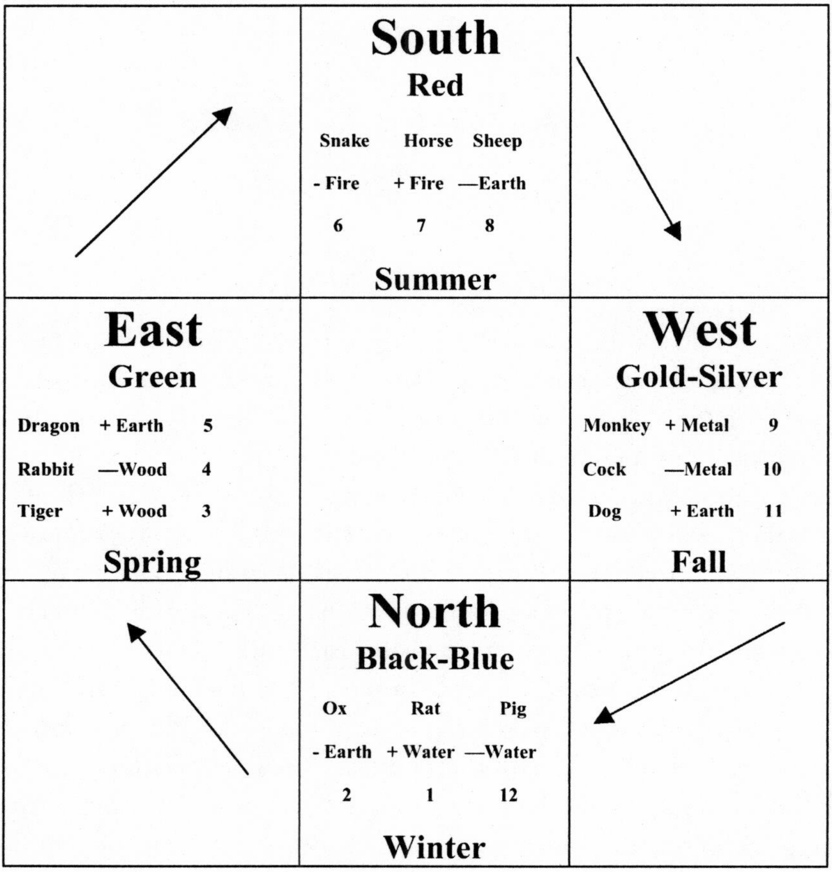

	South	
↗	**Red** Snake　　Horse　Sheep - Fire　　+ Fire　—Earth 6　　　　7　　　8 **Summer**	↘
East **Green** Dragon　+ Earth　5 Rabbit　—Wood　4 Tiger　+ Wood　3 **Spring**		**West** **Gold-Silver** Monkey　+ Metal　9 Cock　—Metal　10 Dog　+ Earth　11 **Fall**
↖	**North** **Black-Blue** Ox　　Rat　　Pig - Earth　+ Water　—Water 2　　　1　　　12 **Winter**	↙

Branch—Animal Relationships

Table 5b summarizes the major relationships of Branches-Animals. Each Branch has an Animal name, corresponding main element, season, time of day and direction. Under the main element is the Chinese name for the Branch. This information is used to calculate specific elemental influences that affect a person. These influences are explained in detail throughout the book.

Table 5b

Animal	Main Element *	Season	Time of Day	Direction
Pig	Yang Water Hai	Winter	9pm-11pm	North
Rat	Yin Water	Winter	11pm-1am	North
Ox	Yin Earth Chou	Winter	1am-3am	North
Tiger	Yang Wood Yin	Spring	3am-5am	East
Rabbit	Yin Wood Mao	Spring	5am-7am	East
Dragon	Yang Earth Chen	Spring	7am-9am	East
Snake	Yang Fire Si	Summer	9am-11am	South
Horse	Yin Fire Wu	Summer	11am-1pm	South
Sheep	Yin Earth Wei	Summer	1pm-3pm	South
Monkey	Yang Metal Shen	Fall	3pm-5pm	West
Cock	Yin Metal Yu	Fall	5pm-7pm	West
Dog	Yang Earth Shu	Fall	7pm-9pm	West

* Reflects the Internal Method.

Finding Branch Gender

F inding Branch gender or polarity is determining whether a Branch is Yin or Yang, this determination is an integral aspect in Four Pillars and Oriental Medicine.

There are two major methods of determining the gender of each Animal. The first is the Outer method and the Second is the Internal Method. The Outer method assists when calculating 10-Year Life Cycles. All other calculations use the Inner Method.

The gender is the same for eight Branches whether the Internal or Outer Method is applied. The following four Branches change their gender: Pig, Rat, Snake and Horse, see the table below.

Branch-Animal	Internal Method	Outer Method
Pig	Yang Water	Yin Water
Rat	Yin Water	Yang Water
Snake	Yang Fire	Yin Fire
Horse	Yin Fire	Yang Fire

Outer Method

I n diagram 5c the main element depicts the Outer method for calculating the Yin-Yang aspect of each Animal or Branch. The concept of numbers and Yin-Yang can elucidate this method. For example, the Rat is 1, Ox-2, Tiger-3, Rabbit-4, Dragon-5, Snake-6, Horse-7, Sheep-8, Monkey-9, Cock-10, Dog-11 and Pig 12, (Diagram 5c). Odd numbers are Yang and even numbers are Yin.

The Outer Method is used to calculate 10-Year Life Cycles (Chapter 8). Diagram 5c reflects this outer approach. The + sign means Yang and the— sign means Yin. For example, if a person was born in a Cock year, they are *Yin* Metal (Cock). If the person is a woman, she is a *Yin Female*, if a man, a *Yin male.*

Diagram 5c

Outer Method

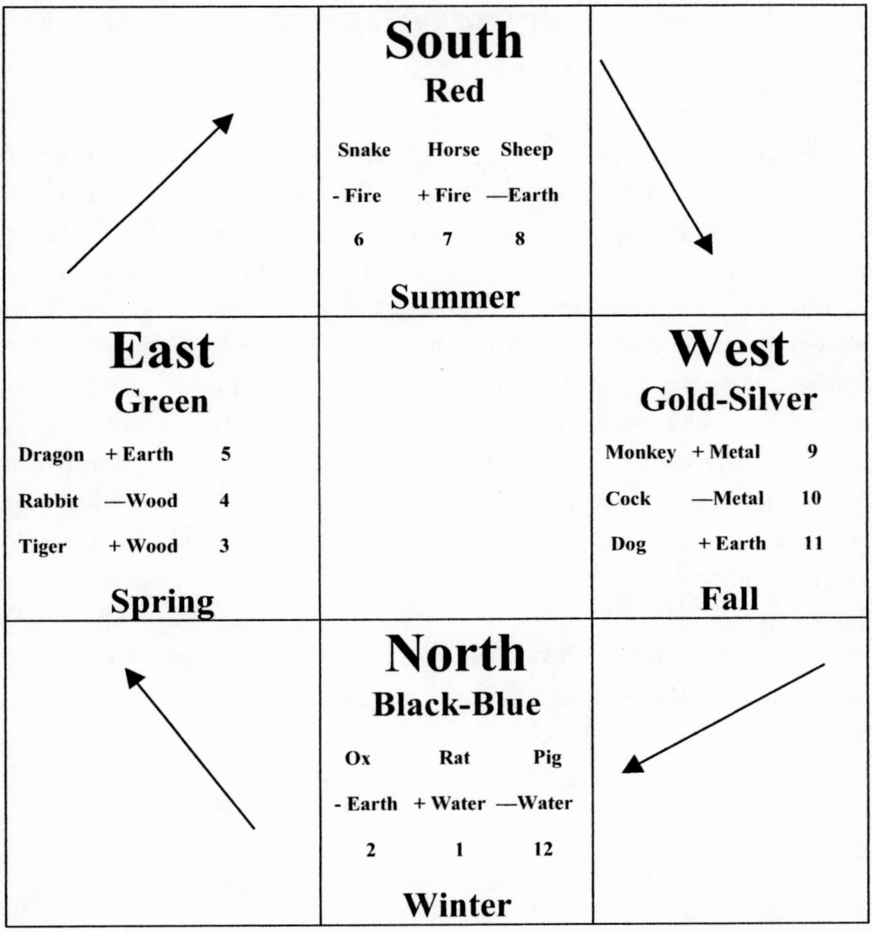

	South **Red** Snake Horse Sheep - Fire + Fire —Earth 6 7 8 **Summer**	
East **Green** Dragon + Earth 5 Rabbit —Wood 4 Tiger + Wood 3 **Spring**		**West** **Gold-Silver** Monkey + Metal 9 Cock —Metal 10 Dog + Earth 11 **Fall**
	North **Black-Blue** Ox Rat Pig - Earth + Water —Water 2 1 12 **Winter**	

Internal Method

I n most applications of the Four Pillars the internal method is used. Each of the Branches, except the four Earths (Ox, Dragon, Sheep and Dog) are Yin-Yang pairs. The Earths are transformers from one season to another and are not considered "pure" aspects of their cardinal position, they are mixtures of numerous elements and unifying forces. This will be explained throughout the book. For each geographical location there is a pair of "pure" branches, the first animal is Yang and the second is Yin. Odd numbers are Yang and even numbers are Yin. For example, North contains Pig-Rat, East contains Tiger-Rabbit, South contains Snake-Horse and West contains Monkey-Cock. The Pig, Tiger, Snake and Monkey are Yang and the Rat, Rabbit, Horse and Cock are Yin, (Diagram 5d). *This formula is used in all calculations except the Yin-Yang gender of the Birth Year when calculating 10-Year Life Cycles. The polarity of the birth year Branch in the Four Pillars is based on the Inner method, as are all Branches.*

Diagram 5d

Internal Method

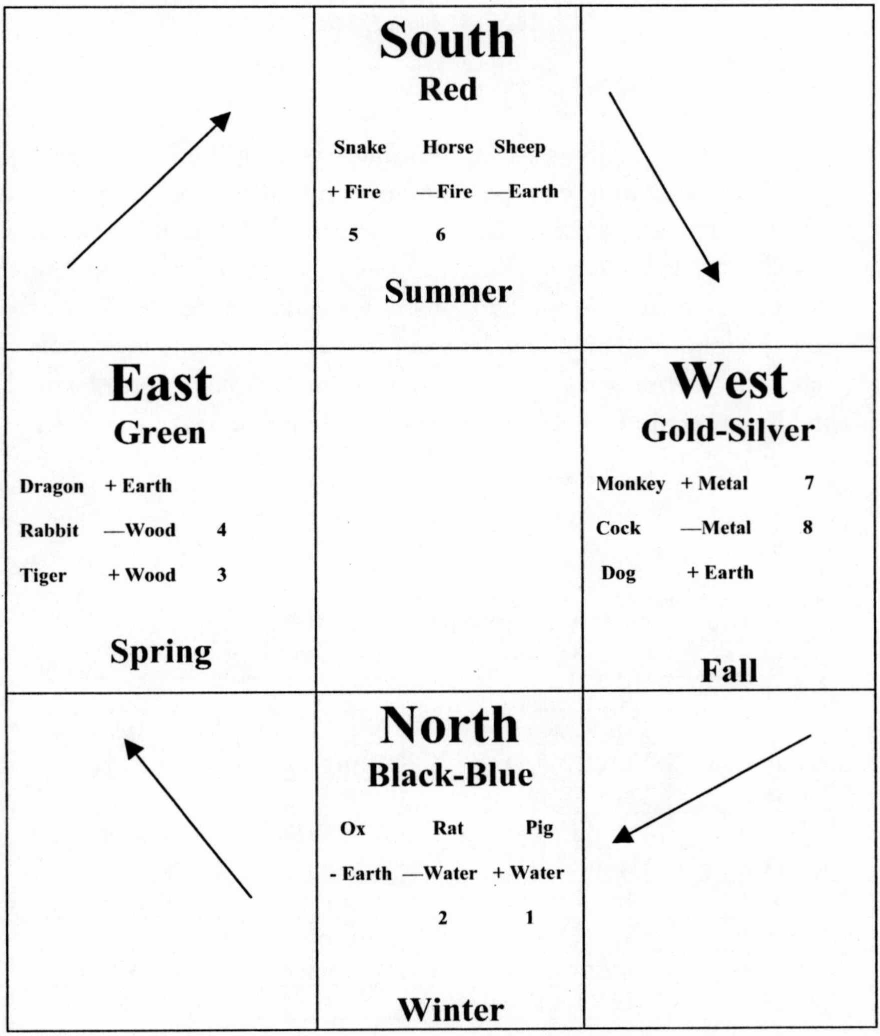

	South **Red** Snake Horse Sheep + Fire —Fire —Earth 5 6 **Summer**	
East **Green** Dragon + Earth Rabbit —Wood 4 Tiger + Wood 3 **Spring**		**West** **Gold-Silver** Monkey + Metal 7 Cock —Metal 8 Dog + Earth **Fall**
	North **Black-Blue** Ox Rat Pig - Earth —Water + Water 2 1 **Winter**	

Hidden Elements

Nine of the 12 Branches or Animals contain "Hidden Elements". These are minor elements contained inside a Branch. The Hidden Elements influence each person and must be thoroughly evaluated. Table 5e shows the Hidden Elements contained in each Animal or Branch. The bottom of each page in the Chinese Calendar Made Easy has a box showing the main and Hidden elements for each Animal. These elements represent the Internal Method and are used for all calculations *except* the polarity of the Year Branch of birth when calculating 10-Year Life Cycles.

Table 5e

Hidden Elements

Animal	Main Element	Hidden Element
Pig	Yang Water	Yang Wood
Rat	Yin Water	
Ox	Yin Earth	Yin Water, Yin Metal
Tiger	Yang Wood	Yang Fire, Yang Earth
Rabbit	Yin Wood	
Dragon	Yang Earth	Yin Wood, Yin Water
Snake	Yang Fire	Yang Earth, Yang Metal
Horse	Yin Fire	Yin Earth
Sheep	Yin Earth	Yin Fire, Yin Wood
Monkey	Yang Metal	Yang Earth, Yang Water
Cock	Yin Metal	
Dog	Yang Earth	Yin Metal, Yin Fire

Chapter 6

Chinese Calendar

The Chinese Calendar is also called the Natural Energy Calendar or the 10,000-Year Calendar. According to legend it began 2698 B.C.; the first day of the first year of Huang Di, the Yellow Emperor's reign. This calendar is the foundation for the Four Pillars. The Chinese Calendar Made Easy ©, incorporates all the necessary elements to calculate an authentic Four Pillars chart, it is used to find the Stem and Branch for any Hour, Day, Month or Year.

The following are six integral components necessary to find correct birth information.

Chinese Age

At birth a person is one year old. When 12 years old in the western calendar, a person is 13 years old in Four Pillars. Always add one to the western birth age. This is important for forecasting the timing of events. This cycle begins on the birthday, *not* the beginning of the New Year.

Daylight Savings Time

Daylight savings time must be adjusted to determine an accurate Four Pillars chart. If daylight savings time was used subtract one hour from the time of birth.

To confirm if daylight savings time was in effect refer to the following book:

Time Changes in the USA, by Doris Doane.
Time Changes in Canada and Mexico, by Doris Doane.
Time Changes in the World, by Doris Doane.

Place of Birth

Use the time of birth in the city in which you were born. Do not convert to China time or any other time zone.

Solar Calendar

The Chinese Calendar Made Easy © is based upon the Solar calendar, not the Lunar calendar.

Day

A new day begins after midnight. The Zi or Rat time is 11:00pm-1:00am. A new day does not begin after 11:00pm.

Hour

The Hour of birth is based on the standard double Chinese hours. For example, the Zi hour includes any time from 11:00pm-1:00am, see Table 7b.

Below is an example explaining how to use the Chinese Calendar Made Easy ©.

1931

Column 1	Column 2		Column 3		Columns 4 5 6		
	Month		Year				
Find Your Day Here	Stem	Branch	Stem	Branch	Day	Day	Time
January 6 – February 5	Yin Earth	Ox	Yang Metal	Horse	Jan	52	14:56
February 5— March 7	Yang Metal	Tiger	Yin Metal	Sheep	Feb	23	2: 41
March 7— April 6	Yin Metal	Rabbit	Yin Metal	Sheep	March	51	21: 03
April 6— May 7	Yang Water	Dragon	Yin Metal	Sheep	April	22	2: 21
May 7 – June 7	Yin Water	Snake	Yin Metal	Sheep	May	52	20: 10
June 7— July 8	Yang Wood	Horse	Yin Metal	Sheep	June	23	: 42
July 8— August 8	Yin Wood	Sheep	Yin Metal	Sheep	July	53	11: 06
August 8— September 9	Yang Fire	Monkey	Yin Metal	Sheep	Aug	24	20: 45
September 9 – October 9	Yin Fire	Cock	Yin Metal	Sheep	Sept	55	23: 18
October 9— November 8	Yang Earth	Dog	Yin Metal	Sheep	Oct	25	14: 27
November 8— December 8	Yin Earth	Pig	Yin Metal	Sheep	Nov	56	17: 10
December 8 – January 6	Yang Metal	Rat	Yin Metal	Sheep	Dec	26	9: 41

Branch	Pig	Rat	Ox	Tiger	Rabbit	Dragon	Snake	Horse	Sheep	Monkey	Cock	Dog
Main Element	Yang Water	Yin Water	Yin Earth	Yang Wood	Yin Wood	Yang Earth	Yin Fire	Yin Fire	Yin Earth	Yang Metal	Yin Metal	Yang Earth
Hidden Elements	Yang Wood		Yin Water	Yang Fire		Yin Wood	Yang Earth	Yin Earth	Yin Fire	Yang Earth		Yin Metal
			Yin Metal	Yang Earth		Yin Water	Yang Metal		Yin Wood	Yang Water		Yin Fire

- Column 1 contains solar days. Locate the day in question here.
- Column 2 is the Stem and Branch for the Month in question. This is the Month Binomial.
- Column 3 is the Year Stem and Branch. This is the Year Binomial.
- *Column 4 and 5 are labeled "Day". These columns are used to find the Day Binomial. Column 4 lists the 12 months. Find the month in question in column 4 and then move to column 5, **column 5 has a special number which is used to assist in finding the Day Binomial.** Add the day in question to this number. The total creates a binomial number. Find the Binomial number in Table 6a.*

Table 6a

Stem and Branch Cycle of 60
For Hours, Days, Months and Years

Number	1	2	3	4	5	6
Stem Branch	Yang Wood Rat	Yin Wood Ox	Yang Fire Tiger	Yin Fire Rabbit	Yang Earth Dragon	Yin Earth Snake
Number	7	8	9	10	11	12
Stem Branch	Yang Metal Horse	Yin Metal Sheep	Yang Water Monkey	Yin Water Cock	Yang Wood Dog	Yin Wood Pig
Number	13	14	15	16	17	18
Stem Branch	Yang Fire Rat	Yin Fire Ox	Yang Earth Tiger	Yin Earth Rabbit	Yang Metal Dragon	Yin Metal Snake
Number	19	20	21	22	23	24
Stem Branch	Yang Water Horse	Yin Water Sheep	Yang Wood Monkey	Yin Wood Cock	Yang Fire Dog	Yin Fire Pig
Number	25	26	27	28	29	30
Stem Branch	Yang Earth Rat	Yin Earth Ox	Yang Metal Tiger	Yin Metal Rabbit	Yang Water Dragon	Yin Water Snake
Number	31	32	33	34	35	36
Stem Branch	Yang Wood Horse	Yin Wood Sheep	Yang Fire Monkey	Yin Fire Cock	Yang Earth Dog	Yin Earth Pig
Number	37	38	39	40	41	42
Stem Branch	Yang Metal Rat	Yin Metal Ox	Yang Water Tiger	Yin Water Rabbit	Yang Wood Dragon	Yin Wood Snake
Number	43	44	45	46	47	48
Stem Branch	Yang Fire Horse	Yin Fire Sheep	Yang Earth Monkey	Yin Earth Cock	Yang Metal Dog	Yin Metal Pig
Number	49	50	51	52	53	54
Stem Branch	Yang Water Rat	Yin Water Ox	Yang Wood Tiger	Yin Wood Rabbit	Yang Fire Dragon	Yin Fire Snake
Number	55	56	57	58	59	60
Stem Branch	Yang Earth Horse	Yin Earth Sheep	Yang Metal Monkey	Yin Metal Cock	Yang Water Dog	Yin Water Pig

Branch	Pig	Rat	Ox	Tiger	Rabbit	Dragon	Snake	Horse	Sheep	Monkey	Cock	Dog
Main Element	Yang Water	Yin Water	Yin Earth	Yang Wood	Yin Wood	Yang Earth	Yang Fire	Yin Fire	Yin Earth	Yang Metal	Yin Metal	Yang Earth

The table above reflects the inner-method.

Example 1

February 10, 1931.

Refer to column 4, locate February and move to column 5. The special number is 23. Add 23 to 10 (February 10) which totals 33. "33" is the Binomial for your Day Stem and Branch. Find number 33, in Table 6.

The Day Binomial is Yang Fire, Monkey.

	Hour	**Day**	**Month**	**Year**
Stem		Yang Fire		
Branch		Monkey ·		

Example 2

September 20, 1931.

The Special Day number is 55. Add 20 (September 20) to 55, the total is 75.

Subtract 60 from 75. The binomial is 15 or Yang Earth, Tiger.

****

The binomial chart has 60 segments. If the total of the day in question and Special Day number for the month is greater than 60, subtract 60 from the total. In this case subtract 60 from 75. The result is 15. Locate 15 in the Day Stem and Branch Table. The binomial must be 1-60. If the combination is greater than 60, subtract 60 from the total, the remainder is the binomial.

****

	Hour	Day	Month	Year
Stem		Yang Earth		
Branch		Tiger		

- Column 6 is the Month Divider time. If your day is on the first day of the solar month this is the exact time the month changes. This is used for the Month Stem and Branch only.

Chapter 7

The Four Pillars

The Four Pillars are Stems and Branches of the Hour, Day, Month and Year of birth; they comprise the constitutional birth chart. The Chinese Calendar Made Easy © contains the information to construct the Four Pillars. The next example illustrates how to calculate the Four Pillars. Use the information below or refer to 1999 in the Appendix.

A Male born January 28, 1999 at 5:30 am.

1999

Find your Day Here	Month Stem	Branch	Year Stem	Branch	Day	Day	Time
January 6 – February 4	Yin Wood	Ox	Yang Earth	Tiger	Jan	49	3: 00
February 4— March 6	Yang Fire	Tiger	Yin Earth	Rabbit	Feb	20	14: 42
March 6 —April 5	Yin Fire	Rabbit	Yin Earth	Rabbit	March	48	8: 52
April 5— May 6	Yang Earth	Dragon	Yin Earth	Rabbit	April	19	13: 55
May 6 – June 6	Yin Earth	Snake	Yin Earth	Rabbit	May	49	7: 29
June 6— July 7	Yang Metal	Horse	Yin Earth	Rabbit	June	20	11: 51
July 7— August 8	Yin Metal	Sheep	Yin Earth	Rabbit	July	50	22: 14
August 8— September 8	Yang Water	Monkey	Yin Earth	Rabbit	Aug	21	7: 57
September 8 – October 9	Yin Water	Cock	Yin Earth	Rabbit	Sept	52	10: 41
October 9— November 7	Yang Wood	Dog	Yin Earth	Rabbit	Oct	22	2: 05
November 7— December 7	Yin Wood	Pig	Yin Earth	Rabbit	Nov	53	5: 01
December 7 – January 6	Yang Fire	Rat	Yin Earth	Rabbit	Dec	23	21: 14

1. Locate the solar day in column 1.

    Move directly to the right and take note of the Month Stem and Branch, in this example Column 2 or Yin Wood, Ox. Place this Binomial in the Four Pillar Chart below.

	Hour	Day	Month	Year
Stem			Yin Wood	
Branch			Ox	

2. Move directly to the right and write down the Year Stem and Branch. Column 3. Yang Earth, Tiger. See Four Pillars below.

	Hour	Day	Month	Year
Stem			Yin Wood	Yang Earth
Branch			Ox	Tiger

3. Move to the right and locate the month in question, January (column 4) and continue to the right to the Day number, take note of the number in the Day Column, Column 5.

Add the day of birth on any day to this number. 49 plus 28 (January 28) = 77. 77-60 = 17, this is the Day Stem and Branch Binomial.

As a reminder, the number in this column assists in finding the Binomial for the Day of birth. There are 60 Binomials or combinations. If the total of the Birthday and the Column Day exceeds 60, subtract 60 from the total. In this example, the total is 77, subtract 60, resulting in Binomial 17.

In the Stem and Branch Cycle of 60 Chart, see table 7a, find Binomial 17, this is the Day Stem and Branch Binomial. It is Yang Metal, Dragon. Place this Binomial in the Four Pillars.

	Hour	Day	Month	Year
Stem		Yang Metal	Yin Wood	Yang Earth
Branch		Dragon	Ox	Tiger

Table 7a

Stem and Branch Cycle of 60
For Hours, Days, Months and Years

Number	1	2	3	4	5	6
Stem Branch	Yang Wood Rat	Yin Wood Ox	Yang Fire Tiger	Yin Fire Rabbit	Yang Earth Dragon	Yin Earth Snake
Number	7	8	9	10	11	12
Stem Branch	Yang Metal Horse	Yin Metal Sheep	Yang Water Monkeyz	Yin Water Cock	Yang Wood Dog	Yin Wood Pig
Number	13	14	15	16	17	18
Stem Branch	Yang Fire Rat	Yin Fire Ox	Yang Earth Tiger	Yin Earth Rabbit	Yang Metal Dragon	Yin Metal Snake
Number	19	20	21	22	23	24
Stem Branch	Yang Water Horse	Yin Water Sheep	Yang Wood Monkey	Yin Wood Cock	Yang Fire Dog	Yin Fire Pig
Number	25	26	27	28	29	30
Stem Branch	Yang Earth Rat	Yin Earth Ox	Yang Metal Tiger	Yin Metal Rabbit	Yang Water Dragon	Yin Water Snake
Number	31	32	33	34	35	36
Stem Branch	Yang Wood Horse	Yin Wood Sheep	Yang Fire Monkey	Yin Fire Cock	Yang Earth Dog	Yin Earth Pig
Number	37	38	39	40	41	42
Stem Branch	Yang Metal Rat	Yin Metal Ox	Yang Water Tiger	Yin Water Rabbit	Yang Wood Dragon	Yin Wood Snake
Number	43	44	45	46	47	48
Stem Branch	Yang Fire Horse	Yin Fire Sheep	Yang Earth Monkey	Yin Earth Cock	Yang Metal Dog	Yin Metal Pig
Number	49	50	51	52	53	54
Stem Branch	Yang Water Rat	Yin Water Ox	Yang Wood Tiger	Yin Wood Rabbit	Yang Fire Dragon	Yin Fire Snake
Number	55	56	57	58	59	60
Stem Branch	Yang Earth Horse	Yin Earth Sheep	Yang Metal Monkey	Yin Metal Cock	Yang Water Dog	Yin Water Pig

Branch	Pig	Rat	Ox	Tiger	Rabbit	Dragon	Snake	Horse	Sheep	Monkey	Cock	Dog
Main Element	Yang Water	Yin Water	Yin Earth	Yang Wood	Yin Wood	Yang Earth	Yang Fire	Yin Fire	Yin Earth	Yang Metal	Yin Metal	Yang Earth

4. Refer to the Hour Stem and Branch Chart, Table 7b; locate the *Day Stem* in the top row and look directly below it to the Stem and Branch that corresponds to the time of birth.

    The Day Stem is Yang Metal, move to 5:30 am which is Yin Earth, Rabbit. This is the Hour Stem and Branch. See below.

Table 7b

Hour Stem and Branch Chart

Day Stem➡	Yang Wood Yin Earth	Yang Metal Yin Wood	Yang Fire Yin Metal	Yang Water Yin Fire	Yang Earth Yin Water
11 pm-1 am	Yang Wood Rat	Yang Fire Rat	Yang Earth Rat	Yang Metal Rat	Yang Water Rat
1 am-3 am	Yin Wood Ox	Yin Fire Ox	Yin Earth Ox	Yin Metal Ox	Yin Water Ox
3 am-5 am	Yang Fire Tiger	Yang Earth Tiger	Yang Metal Tiger	Yang Water Tiger	Yang Wood Tiger
5 am-7 am	Yin Fire Rabbit	Yin Earth Rabbit	Yin Metal Rabbit	Yin Water Rabbit	Yin Wood Rabbit
7 am-9 am	Yang Earth Dragon	Yang Metal Dragon	Yang Water Dragon	Yang Wood Dragon	Yang Fire Dragon
9 am-11 am	Yin Earth Snake	Yin Metal Snake	Yin Water Snake	Yin Wood Snake	Yin Fire Snake
11 am-1 pm	Yang Metal Horse	Yang Water Horse	Yang Wood Horse	Yang Fire Horse	Yang Earth Horse
1 pm-3 pm	Yin Metal Sheep	Yin Water Sheep	Yin Wood Sheep	Yin Fire Sheep	Yin Earth Sheep
3 pm-5 pm	Yang Water Monkey	Yang Wood Monkey	Yang Fire Monkey	Yang Earth Monkey	Yang Metal Monkey
5 pm-7 pm	Yin Water Cock	Yin Wood Cock	Yin Fire Cock	Yin Earth Cock	Yin Metal Cock
7 pm- 9 pm	Yang Wood Dog	Yang Fire Dog	Yang Earth Dog	Yang Metal Dog	Yang Water Dog
9 pm-11 pm	Yin Wood Pig	Yin Fire Pig	Yin Earth Pig	Yin Metal Pig	Yin Water Pig

Four Pillars

	Hour	Day	Month	Year
Stem	Yin Earth	Yang Metal	Yin Wood	Yang Earth
Branch	Rabbit	Dragon	Ox	Tiger

Example

F ind the Four Pillars for the following person and confirm your cal-culations. The following is a step by step process for calculating the Four Pillars.

Male born on June 30, 1957.
6:30 am daylight savings time.

1.   Locate the Year in question in the Chinese Calendar Made Easy ©, see Table 7c.
2.   Locate the day in question in column 1.
3.   Column 2 is the Month Stem and Branch.
4.   Column 3 is the Year Stem and Branch.
5.   Locate the month in question in Column 4; locate the Day number in column 5. Add the day in question to this number, the result is the Day Binomial. Refer to the Stem and Branch Cycle of 60 and locate the Binomial. This is the Day Stem and Branch.
6.   Refer to the Hour Stem and Branch chart, find the Day Stem in the top row and move down until the time of birth. This is the Hour Stem and Branch.

Table 7c

1957

	Month		Year		
Find your Day Here	**Stem**	**Branch**	**Stem**	**Branch**	**Day**
January 5 – February 4	Yin Metal	Ox	Yang Fire	Monkey	4
February 4— March 6	Yang Water	Tiger	Yin Fire	Cock	40
March 6— April 5	Yin Water	Rabbit	Yin Fire	Cock	8
April 5— May 6	Yang Wood	Dragon	Yin Fire	Cock	39
May 6—June 6	Yin Wood	Snake	Yin Fire	Cock	9
June 6— July 7	Yang Fire	Horse	Yin Fire	Cock	40
July 7— August 8	Yin Fire	Sheep	Yin Fire	Cock	10
August 8— September 8	Yang Earth	Monkey	Yin Fire	Cock	41
September 8—October 8	Yin Earth	Cock	Yin Fire	Cock	12
October 8— November 8	Yang Metal	Dog	Yin Fire	Cock	42
November 8— December 7	Yin Metal	Pig	Yin Fire	Cock	13
December 7—January 6	Yang Water	Rat	Yin Fire	Cock	43

Male born on June 30, 1957, at 6:30 am, Boston, Massachusetts

Four Pillars

	Hour	**Day**	**Month**	**Year**
Stem	Yin Wood	Yin Water	Yang Fire	Yin Fire
Branch	Rabbit	Cock	Horse	Cock
Elements	Yin Wood	Yin Metal	Yin Fire Yin Earth	Yin Metal

Chapter 8

10 Year Life Cycles

Ten-Year Life Cycles are Stem and Branch influences during 10-Year segments throughout one's lifetime. These cycles combine with the Four Pillars to create post-natal health influences. When favorable cycles occur, health is positively influenced. Conversely, when unfavorable elements enter a new cycle, health is negatively influenced. Ten-Year Life Cycles represent nature's variable or dynamic influences.

Ten-Year Life Cycles are more influential than Day, Month or Yearly cycles. Evaluating the conditions of the Four Pillars and the influences of 10-Year Life Cycles provides a complete picture of how nature influences a person's health, the diagram below illustrates this phenomenon.

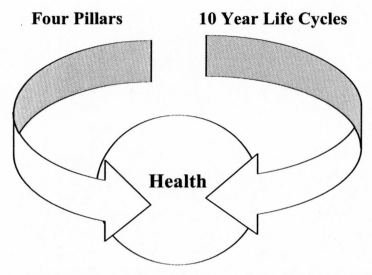

The combination of the Four Pillars and 10-Yeal Life Cycles reflect the changing aspect of nature and connects pre-natal and post-natal influences.

Calculating 10 Year Life Cycles

1.   Determine if the person is Male or Female.

2.   Identify the polarity of the Year of birth Branch and note whether the main Element is Yin or Yang, use the Outer Method. The following table lists the Elements for this calculation.

Branch polarity for calculating 10-Year Life Cycles.

Branch	*Main Element
Pig	Yin Water
Rat	Yang Water
Ox	Yin Earth
Tiger	Yang Wood
Rabbit	Yin Wood
Dragon	Yang Earth
Snake	Yin Fire
Horse	Yang Fire
Sheep	Yin Earth
Monkey	Yang Metal
Cock	Yin Metal
Dog	Yang Earth

* The polarity is based on the Outer-Method.

3.   Yin Females count (move) forward in time, for example, Pig, Ox, Rabbit, Snake, Sheep and Cock.
Yang Females count (move) backward in time, for example, Rat, Tiger, Dragon, Horse, Monkey and Dog.

Yang Males count (move) forward in time, for example, Rat, Tiger, Dragon, Horse, Monkey and Dog.

Yin Males count (move) backward in time, for example, Pig, Ox, Rabbit, Snake, Sheep and Cock.

4.   Locate the birthday in column 1 of the Chinese Calendar Made Easy ©.

5.   If the person is a Yin Female or Yang Male, move forward and count the number of days from the Birthday to the end of the solar month (column 1). This is moving forward in time. Use the birthday as the first day counted and the last solar day as a marker. Do not count the last day. When counting forward the last day is never counted.

6.   If the person is a Yang Female or Yin Male move backward and count the number of days from the birthday to the first day of the solar month (column 1), which is backward in time. Use the birthday as the first day counted and do count the first day of the solar month. When counting backward the first day of the month is always counted.

For example, March 15, 1940.

1940 is the Dragon-Yang Earth.

The dividers are March 6 – April 5.

If this person is Female, she is a Yang Dragon Earth, Yang Females count backwards from March 15 to March 6, which is 10 days. We do count March 15, the Birthday, and March 6, the first day in the solar month.

If this person is Male, he is a Yang Dragon, Yang Males count forward from March 15 to April 5. Count the birthday, but not April 5.

***To assist in counting days, refer to the "Counting the 10-Year Life Cycles". The first month is 31 days, 2nd is 30 days, 3rd is 30 days, 4th is 31 days, 5th is 30 and 6th is 28 days. Circle the birthday and the beginning or ending day of the month. Count from the day in question to the beginning or ending day. Be very attentive about the number of days in the month; for example, are there 28, 29, 30 or 31 days in the month?

Counting 10 Year Life Cycles

1	2	3	4	5	6	7	8	9	10	11	12	13	14	15	16	17	18	19	20
21	22	23	24	25	26	27	28	29	30	*31*	1	2	3	4	5	6	7	8	9
10	11	12	13	14	15	16	17	18	19	20	21	22	23	24	25	26	27	28	29
30	1	2	3	4	5	6	7	8	9	10	11	12	13	14	15	16	17	18	19
20	21	22	23	24	25	26	27	28	29	*30*	1	2	3	4	5	6	7	8	9
10	11	12	13	14	15	16	17	18	19	20	21	22	23	24	25	26	27	28	29
30	*31*	1	2	3	4	5	6	7	8	9	10	11	12	13	14	15	16	17	18
19	20	21	22	23	24	25	26	27	28	29	*30*	1	2	3	4	5	6	7	8
9	10	11	12	13	14	15	16	17	18	19	20	21	22	23	24	25	26	27	28

7. Divide the total number of days counted by 3. Ex. 10 days divided by 3 = 3, with a remainder of 1. *3 is the number used.*

Remainder guidelines

In other situations the remainder is 0 or 2. The guidelines are:

1) If the remainder is 0, use the original number.
2) If the remainder is 1, use the original number.
3) If the remainder is 2, round up one number. For example, if the number was 11, divide 11 by 3 to obtain 3, with a remainder of 2. Round up to 4. *4 becomes the number utilzed.*

The reason for this application is:

1. Each day counted represents four months or 33% of one year.
2. Two days represent eight months, or 66% of a year and is rounded up to the next number.

When the percentage of months is greater than 50%, the number is rounded up.

When the number of days counted is two days or less, use the following method:

If the number of days is 2, the 10 Year Cycles are 1, 11, 21, 31, 41, 51, etc.

If the number of days is 1, the 10 Year Cycles are 1, 11, 21, 31, 41, 51, etc.

If born on the first or last solar day, in other words there are 0 days counted, begin the first 10-Year Luck Cycle at birth. For example,
0, 10, 20, 30, 40, 50, 60, 70, 80, 90.

The Month pillar is the Stem and Branch influence used for the time period from Birth to the first 10-Year Life Cycle. The Month pillar is the Parent pillar and has the most influence during childhood.

8.   Write numbers left to right.

The first 10-Year Life Cycle begins with the number calculated. In this case 3.

0   3   13   23   33   43   53   63   73   83   93   103

These represent 10-Year Cycles throughout a life.

In this case, 0-2 years old is the Month Stem and Branch in the Four Pillars.

9.   Finding the Stem and Branch for 10-Year Life Cycles.

A *Yin Female* or *Yang Male* moves forward. Refer to the 60 Stem and Branch cycle chart and find the *Birth Month Stem and Branch Binomial,* place this in age 0. Move forward to the next binomial and place it in the first 10-Year Cycle. Continue to the next binomial and place it in the following 10-Year cycle. Continue this process for as many cycles as you prefer.

A *Yang Female* and *Yin Male* moves backwards. Refer to the 60 Stem and Branch cycle chart and find the *Birth Month Stem and Branch Binomial,* place it in age 0. Move to the preceding binomial and place it in the first 10-Year cycle. Continue moving backwards to the next binomial and place it in the following 10 Year cycle. Continue this process for as many cycles as you prefer.

Summary

Type	Method of Counting 10 Year Life cycles
Yin Female or Yang Male	Count forward from the Birthday to the end of the solar month. *Do not* count the last solar day.
Yang Female or Yin Male	Count backwards from the Birthday to the first day of the solar month. *Do* count the first day of the solar month.
	In both cases *do* count the Birthday.

Stem and Branch Cycle of 60
For Hours, Days, Months and Years

Number	1	2	3	4	5	6
Stem	Yang Wood	Yin Wood	Yang Fire	Yin Fire	Yang Earth	Yin Earth
Branch	Rat	Ox	Tiger	Rabbit	Dragon	Snake
Number	7	8	9	10	11	12
Stem	Yang Metal	Yin Metal	Yang Water	Yin Water	Yang Wood	Yin Wood
Branch	Horse	Sheep	Monkey	Cock	Dog	Pig
Number	13	14	15	16	17	18
Stem	Yang Fire	Yin Fire	Yang Earth	Yin Earth	Yang Metal	Yin Metal
Branch	Rat	Ox	Tiger	Rabbit	Dragon	Snake
Number	19	20	21	22	23	24
Stem	Yang Water	Yin Water	Yang Wood	Yin Wood	Yang Fire	Yin Fire
Branch	Horse	Sheep	Monkey	Cock	Dog	Pig
Number	25	26	27	28	29	30
Stem	Yang Earth	Yin Earth	Yang Metal	Yin Metal	Yang Water	Yin Water
Branch	Rat	Ox	Tiger	Rabbit	Dragon	Snake
Number	31	32	33	34	35	36
Stem	Yang Wood	Yin Wood	Yang Fire	Yin Fire	Yang Earth	Yin Earth
Branch	Horse	Sheep	Monkey	Cock	Dog	Pig
Number	37	38	39	40	41	42
Stem	Yang Metal	Yin Metal	Yang Water	Yin Water	Yang Wood	Yin Wood
Branch	Rat	Ox	Tiger	Rabbit	Dragon	Snake
Number	43	44	45	46	47	48
Stem	Yang Fire	Yin Fire	Yang Earth	Yin Earth	Yang Metal	Yin Metal
Branch	Horse	Sheep	Monkey	Cock	Dog	Pig
Number	49	50	51	52	53	54
Stem	Yang Water	Yin Water	Yang Wood	Yin Wood	Yang Fire	Yin Fire
Branch	Rat	Ox	Tiger	Rabbit	Dragon	Snake
Number	55	56	57	58	59	60
Stem	Yang Earth	Yin Earth	Yang Metal	Yin Metal	Yang Water	Yin Water
Branch	Horse	Sheep	Monkey	Cock	Dog	Pig

Branch	Pig	Rat	Ox	Tiger	Rabbit	Dragon	Snake	Horse	Sheep	Monkey	Cock	Dog
Main Element	Yang Water	Yin Water	Yin Earth	Yang Wood	Yin Wood	Yang Earth	Yang Fire	Yin Fire	Yin Earth	Yang Metal	Yin Metal	Yang Earth
Hidden Element	Yang Wood		Yin Water	Yang Fire		Yin Wood	Yang Earth	Yin Earth	Yin Fire	Yang Earth		Yin Metal
			Yin Metal	Yang Earth		Yin Water	Yang Metal		Yin Wood	Yang Water		Yin Fire

Example

A male born on June 30, 1957 at 6:30 am daylight savings time.

Four Pillars

	Hour	Day	Month	Year
Stem	Yin Wood	Yin Water	Yang Fire	Yin Fire
Branch	Rabbit	Cock	Horse	Cock
Elements	Yin Wood	Yin Metal	Yin Fire Yin Earth	Yin Metal

10 Year Life Cycles

Age	0	8	18	28	38	48	58	68	78
Stem	Yang Fire	Yin Wood	Yang Wood	Yin Water	Yang Water	Yin Metal	Yang Metal	Yin Earth	Yang Earth
Branch	Horse	Snake	Dragon	Rabbit	Tiger	Ox	Rat	Pig	Dog
Main Element	Yin Fire	Yang Fire	Yang Earth	Yin Wood	Yang Wood	Yin Earth	Yin Water	Yang Water	Yang Earth
Hidden Elements	Yin Earth	Yang Earth Yang Metal	Yin Wood Yin Water		Yang Fire Yang Earth	Yin Water Yin Metal		Yang Wood	Yin Metal Yin Fire

The birthday is June 30, 1957. This is Yin Cock or Yin Male, count backwards. The solar month is June 6—July 7. Count from June 30 to

June 6. *Include the first solar day and the birthday.* There are 25 days. Divide 25 by 3 to get 8 with a remainder of 1. Do not round up, use 8. Eight years to 17 years is the first 10-Year Life Cycle. See example above.

The Month Stem and Branch is Yang Fire/Horse or number 43 in the 60 Stem and Branch Cycle Chart, place this in the 0 time frame. This is a Yin Male, move backward. Place Binomial 42, Yin Wood, Snake in the first 10 Year cycle, which is the 8-17 cycle, place Binomial 41 in the 18-27 cycle, continue for as many 10 year cycles as you prefer.

Chapter 9

Stem Transformations

One of the underlying principles in Oriental Medicine is change. The Five Element qualities of Stems change with specific combinations. It is like mixing colors together. Certain colors combine to create a new color. When certain elements mix, they convert into a new, single element. Transformation occurs under specific conditions.

Transformations can occur in the Four Pillars, 10-Year Life Cycles, Yearly or Monthly time frames. If the transformation occurs in the Four Pillars, the change exists for a lifetime. If an element from a future cycle of time combines with an element in the Four Pillars, the transformation lasts for the duration of the cycle of time. When the time frame ends, the transformed element reverts back to its original element. For example, it takes two stems to cause a transformation, if one is in the Four Pillars and one appears in a particular year, the transformation occurs for that year. After the year the new element reverts back to the original element.

A favorable health influence is when a new transformed element benefits the Four-Pillar condition.

An unfavorable health influence is when a new transformed element hinders the Four Pillar chart.

The following are Stem transformations.

Stem Combinations	Transforms into this New Element
Yang Wood and Yin Earth	Earth
Yang Metal and Yin Wood	Metal
Yang Fire and Yin Metal	Water
Yang Water and Yin Fire	Wood
Yang Earth and Yin Water	Fire

Each transformation includes the controlling Five Element relationship. For example, Wood controls Earth and Metal controls Wood. The controlling element is always Yang and the element controlled is always Yin.

Yang Fire combines with Yin Metal. See example 9a.

Example 9a

	Hour	Day	Month	Year
Stem	**Yang Water**	**Yin Water**	*Yang Fire*	*Yin Metal*
Branch				

Yang Fire and Yin Metal transform into Water. View them both as Water See example 9b.

Example 9b

	Hour	Day	Month	Year
Stem	**Yang Water**	**Yin Water**	*Water*	*Water*
Branch				

Yang Wood and Yin Earth transform into Earth, view both as Earth, see examples 9c and 9d.

Example 9c

	Hour	Day	Month	Year
Stem	**Yin Earth**	**Yin Metal**	*Yang Wood*	*Yin Earth*
Branch				

Example 9d

	Hour	Day	Month	Year
Stem	**Yin Earth**	**Yin Metal**	*Earth*	*Earth*
Branch				

Transformation Rules

Transformations occur under specific conditions and all conditions must exist. These conditions are for Stems in the Four Pillars. Transformations can also occur when Day, Month, Year and 10-Year Cycle Stems combine with Stems in the Four Pillars; in this case they can transform with any of the Stems in the Four Pillars.

1.   *In the Four Pillars Stems combine only when they are next to each other. They must be adjacent.* See examples 9a-9d. In these examples, the Month and Year Stems transform. If the Four Pillar chart was Example 9e. The Hour Stem and Year Stem would not transform, they are not adjacent.

Example 9e

	Hour	Day	Month	Year
Stem	*Yang Wood*	*Yin Metal*	*Yang Water*	*Yin Earth*
Branch				

2.   If the Month and Year Stems have a transformation combination find which element would be the new element. *Look at the Month Branch, if the Month Branch provides Root, which means it is the same element as the new transformed element, then the transformation will occur. This Root provides the support to transform the new element. This Root can be a main or Hidden element.* Refer to example 9f-9g.

Example 9f

Four Pillars

	Hour	Day	Month	Year
Stem	**Yin Wood**	**Yin Water**	*Yang Fire*	*Yin Metal*
Branch	**Rabbit**	**Cock**	**Pig**	**Cock**
Elements	**Yin Wood**	**Yin Metal**	**Yang Water** **Yang Wood**	**Yin Metal**

Example 9g
Transforms to this Chart

	Hour	Day	Month	Year
Stem	**Yin Wood**	**Yin Water**	**Yang Water**	**Yang Water**
Branch	**Rabbit**	**Cock**	**Pig**	**Cock**
Elements	**Yin Wood**	**Yin Metal**	**Yang Water** **Yang Wood**	**Yin Metal**

In 9f the Yang Fire in the Month Stem combines with the Yin Metal in the Year Stem, transforming to Water. *For the transformation to occur the Month Branch must provide Root. The Month Branch is Pig, it contains Yang Water and Yang Wood. The Yang Water provides a Main Root, because it is the main element of the Pig. This Root is the catalyst for the transformation;* it allows it to occur. Example 9g reflects the new transformed element.

****

When a Stem transforms it must have a polarity or gender. The rule is both transformed Stems take on the gender of the element of the Month Branch that provided root. In example 9f, the new Stems take on the gender of the Pig, that is Yang Water. Yang becomes the polarity or gender of both Stems, example 9g.

****

Chapter 10

Determining the Condition of the Five Elements

D
etermining the condition of each element within the Four Pillars
is an art and science. The following is a quantitative method for
calculating the strength of each element. In a short period of
time you will be able to calculate their condition by understanding the
Five Element relationships of the Four Pillars. This formula is very accurate, but no formula is 100% accurate. The key is to understand the
mechanics of the formula and learn to apply the principles without the
formula. The formula does not consider the influence of the location,
meaning how close the element is to the Day Stem and how the elements
influence each other based on proximity. The following explains this procedure and examples follow which illustrate the process.

The following is a method to determine the relative strength of each element in the Four Pillars:

1. Allocate the value of 100 to each of the Stems in the Four Pillars.
2. In Table 10a locate the Element value in each of the Branches of the
   Four Pillars. Include the Hidden Elements.
3. Determine the 12 Stage Growth Cycle for each Element. Table 10b
   contains percentage strengths for each stage. The introduction to
   Table 10a explains this procedure.
4. Multiply the element values found in step 2 by the percentages found
   in step 3, this is the relative strength of each element.

Hidden Elements

Nine of the 12 Branches or Animals contain "Hidden Elements", they are minor elements inside a Branch. The Hidden Elements influence each person and must be evaluated. The Hidden Element chart shows the influence or strength of the main and Hidden Elements, they are fixed values. The bottom of each page in the Chinese Calendar Made Easy is a box showing the main and Hidden Elements.

Table 10a

Hidden Elements
(Relative Weights)

Animal	Main Element		Hidden Element
Pig	Yang Water	70	Yang Wood 30
Rat	Yin Water	100	
Ox	Yin Earth	60	Yin Water 20, Yin Metal 20
Tiger	Yang Wood	60	Yang Fire 20, Yang Earth 20
Rabbit	Yin Wood	100	
Dragon	Yang Earth	60	Yin Wood 20, Yin Water 20
Snake	Yang Fire	60	Yang Earth 20, Yang Metal 20
Horse	Yin Fire	70	Yin Earth 30
Sheep	Yin Earth	60	Yin Fire 20, Yin Wood 20
Monkey	Yang Metal	60	Yang Earth 20, Yang Water 20
Cock	Yin Metal	100	
Dog	Yang Earth	60	Yin Metal 20, Yin Fire 20

12 Stage Growth Cycle

The 12 Stage Growth cycle is a more detailed variation of the Yin-Yang and Five Element cycles of expansion, peaking, decline and regeneration or Waxing and Waning. In this analysis each element in the Four Pillars is compared to the element and energy of the Month Branch; the Month Branch reflects the Season of birth. Each element represents a season and each season may nourish, support, weaken or control another element. This formula clearly illustrates how the Month Branch influences each of the elements in the Four Pillars. The following table shows each element and their corresponding season.

Element	Season
Wood	Spring
Fire	Summer
Earth	Indian Summer or the Transition times from Season to Season
Metal	Fall
Water	Winter

Table 10a contains standard values for elements contained within each Branch. *The 12 Stage Growth Cycle determines the actual degree of strength for those standard values. It is the Month Branch and its Seasonal Five Element influence that determines the relative values.*

How to use Table 10b.

1. In the top row locate each Element in the Four Pillars.
2. Locate the Month Branch from the Four Pillars in the column directly beneath each element. The intersection box of the Element and Month Branch contains the percentage or strength of the 12 Stage Growth Cycle. Use this percentage and multiply it by the Relative weights found in Table 10a. The total is the strength of each element.

Table 10b

12 Stage Growth Cycle

Cycle Stage		Wood	Fire	Earth	Metal	Water
		Element ▼	Element ▼	Element ▼	Element ▼	
1	Birth	Pig 80 %	Tiger 80 %	Tiger 50%	Snake 80%	Monkey 80%
2	Childhood	Rat 50%	Rabbit 50%	Rabbit 50%	Horse 50%	Cock 50%
3	Adolescence	Ox 50 %	Dragon 50%	Dragon 100%	Sheep 50%	Dog 50%
4	Adulthood	Tiger 100%	Snake 100%	Snake 100%	Monkey 100%	Pig 100%
5	Prime	Rabbit 100%	Horse 100%	Horse 100%	Cock 100%	Rat 100%
6	Decline	Dragon 80%	Sheep 80%	Sheep 100%	Dog 80%	Ox 80%
7	Aging	Snake 50%	Monkey 50%	Monkey 50%	Pig 50%	Tiger 50%
8	Death	Horse 50%	Cock 50%	Cock 50%	Rat 50%	Rabbit 50%
9	Dormancy	Sheep 80%	Dog 80%	Dog 100%	Ox 80%	Dragon 80%
10	Void	Monkey 50%	Pig 50%	Pig 50%	Tiger 50%	Snake 50%
11	Embryo	Cock 50%	Rat 50%	Rat 50%	Rabbit 50%	Horse 50%
12	Pregnancy	Dog 50%	Ox 50%	Ox 100%	Dragon 50%	Sheep 50%

Find the Month Branch here

Example 10c
Male born on June 30, 1957 at 6:30 am daylight savings time.

Four Pillars

	Hour	Day	Month	Year
Stem	Yin Wood Offspring 100 X 50%	Yin Water	Yang Fire Grandchild 100 X 100%	Yin Fire Grandchild 100 X 100%
Branch	Rabbit	Cock	Horse	Cock
Elements	Yin Wood Offspring 100 X 50%	Yin Metal Parent 100 X 50%	Yin Fire Grandchild 70 X 100% Yin Earth Grandparent 30 X 50%	Yin Metal Parent 100 X 50%

Element	Relative Strength	Percentage
Metal	100	19%
Water	50	9%
Wood	100	19%
Fire	270	50%
Earth	15	3%

Chapter 11

Stems, Branches and Oriental Medicine

The Four Pillars, which contains four Heavenly Stems and four Earthly Branches can be applied to Oriental Medicine, specifically internal organs, acupuncture channels and areas of the body. Stems, Branches and the condition of the Day Master create the foundation for evaluating the prenatal condition of a person. Each Stem and Branch relates to an internal organ and acupuncture channel. When Stems and Branches or their corresponding Five Elements are in balance there is harmony and health. When Five Elements are deficient or in excess, disharmony or disease is present or is likely to manifest. Tables 11a and 11b lists each Stem and Branch and their related organ. To create a Four Pillars birth chart connect the Stems and Branches from the Four Pillars to their related organs.

Table 11a

Stems	Related Organ -Channel-Area
Yang Wood – Jia	Gallbladder
Yin Wood – Yi	Liver
Yang Fire – Bing	Small Intestine
Yin Fire – Ding	Heart
Yang Earth – Wu	Stomach, Flank-Rib Cage Area
Yin Earth – Ji	Spleen, Abdomen
Yang Metal – Geng	Large Intestine, Navel Area
Yin Metal – Xin	Lungs, Buttocks
Yang Water – Ren	Urinary Bladder, Shins
Yin Water—Kui	Kidney, Lower Limb-Feet

Table 11b

Branches-Animals	Organ-Channel-Area
Pig contains Yang Water	Urinary Bladder, Head, Scrotum, Feet
Rat contains Yin Water	Kidney, Genitals
Ox contains Yin Earth	Spleen, Abdomen, Feet
Tiger contains Yang Wood	Gallbladder, Hair, Hands, Legs
Rabbit contains Yin Wood	Liver, Fingers, Flank
Dragon contains Yang Earth	Stomach, Shoulders, Chest
Snake contains Yang Fire	Small Intestine, Face, Throat, Teeth, Genitals Anus
Horse contains Yin Fire	Heart, Eyes, Head
Sheep contains Yin Earth	Spleen, Diaphragm, Spine
Monkey contains Yang Metal	Large Intestine, Nerves
Cock contains Yin Metal	Lung, Sperm, Blood, Thorax
Dog contains Yang Earth	Stomach, Legs, Ankles, Feet

Four Pillar Constitutional Condition

Determining the condition of a Four Pillars chart is a three-step process.

1. Calculate the Four Pillars. Example 11c.
2. Determine the relative condition of each internal organ in the Four Pillars. Example 11c.
3. Determine favorable and unfavorable elements. Example 11c.
   Favorable elements include elements that supplement weak, reduce excess or bring balance to elements.
   Unfavorable elements are elements that alter balanced, reduce deficient or supplement excessive elements.

   Once these steps are completed the prenatal condition has been determined, energetic conditions of the organs-channels have been revealed and favorable and unfavorable elements identified. Constitutional and predisposed health conditions can be predicted.

Example 11c

Four Pillars

	Hour	Day	Month	Year
Stem	Yin Wood Liver 100X 50%	Yin Water Kidney 100 X 50%	Yang Fire Small Intestine 100 X 100%	Yin Fire Heart 100 X 100%
Branch	Rabbit	Cock	Horse	Cock
Elements	Yin Wood Liver 100 X 50%	Yin Metal Lung 100 X 50%	Yin Fire Heart 70 X 100% Yin Earth Spleen 30 X 50%	Yin Metal Lung 100 X 50%

Element	Organ	Relative Strength	Total Element	Percentage	Condition
Water	Kidney	50	50	9%	Weak
Wood	Liver	100	100	19%	Balanced
Fire	Small Intestine Heart	100 170	270	50%	Excess
Earth	Spleen	15	15	3%	Weak
Metal	Lung	100	100	19%	Balanced

Favorable Elements:
- *Water* controls excess Fire.
- *Metal* is weakened by Fire. Metal supports Metal.
- *Earth* is deficient. Earth supports Earth.

Unfavorable Elements: Fire, Wood-it makes Fire stronger.

- Fire is very excessive; more Fire creates very unfavorable health influences.
- Wood is balanced; it is the resource or parent to Fire, more Wood will increase Fire.

Chapter 12

Day Master

In Four Pillars of Destiny or Tzu Ping Chinese Astrology, the Day Stem is referred to as the Day Master or Self. It is the centerpiece of the Four Pillars and the basis of Astrology. The application of the Day Master in Four Pillars for Health reveals the type of illnesses a person may be predisposed. Specifically, whether a person is more susceptible to acute or chronic conditions.

The method to calculate the condition of the Day Stem is a three-step process.

1. Identify the element of the Day Stem and add the relative values of the Day Stem element and its Resource or Parent element. For example, if the Day Stem element is Wood, the Resource or Parent element is Water. Water and Wood, The Resource and Day Stem element are the strengthening elements. The Child, Grandchild and Controller are the weakening elements. In this example they are Fire, Metal and Earth. Table 12a summarizes all relationships.

    Do not include the Day Stem element in these calculations. *Do* include the element of the Day Stem if found in any other location in the Four Pillars.

2. Total the values of the strengthening and weakening elements.

3. If the strengthening elements exceed the weakening elements, the Day Stem is strong. If the weakening elements exceed the strengthening elements, the Day Stem is weak.

Table 12a

Day Stem Element	Strengthening Elements	Weakening Elements
Water	Metal, Water	Wood, Fire, Earth
Wood	Water, Wood	Fire, Earth, Metal
Fire	Wood, Fire	Earth, Metal, Water
Earth	Fire, Earth	Metal, Water, Wood
Metal	Earth, Metal	Water, Wood, Fire

Day Master Transformations

The Day Stem requires special conditions for a transformation. All conditions must exist for a Day Stem transformation. The following are the conditions.

1. The Day Stem combines only with the Hour Stem or Month Stem, the adjacent Pillars.
2. The new element formed by the transformation must have root in the Month Branch.
3. If the Day Stem element is also in the Hour, Month or Year Stems, there *can not* be a transformation.
4. The grandparent element of the new Transformed Element cannot be anywhere in the Four Pillars. This includes Stems or main elements within the Branches.

The following table summarizes each of the Day Stem transformations.

Day Stem Transformations

Element Combination	New Element	Month Branch (these must be present)
Yang Metal & Yin Wood	Metal	Ox, Snake, Monkey or Cock
Yang Wood & Yin Earth	Earth	Ox, Dragon, Sheep or Dog
Yang Fire & Yin Metal	Water	Rat, Dragon, Monkey or Pig
Yang Water & Yin Fire	Wood	Tiger, Rabbit, Sheep or Pig
Yang Earth & Yin Water	Fire	Tiger, Snake, Horse or Dog

Example

Male born on June 30, 1957 and 6:30 am, daylight savings time.

Four Pillars

	Hour	Day	Month	Year
Stem	Yin Wood Liver 100X 50%	Yin Water Kidney 100 X 50%	Yang Fire Small Intestine 100 X 100%	Yin Fire Heart 100 X 100%
Branch	Rabbit	Cock	Horse	Cock
Elements	Yin Wood Liver 100 X 50%	Yin Metal Lung 100 X 50%	Yin Fire Heart 70 X 100% Yin Earth Spleen 30 X 50%	Yin Metal Lung 100 X 50%

10 Year Life Cycles

Age	0	8	18	28	38	48	58	68	78
Stem	Yang Fire	Yin Wood	Yang Wood	Yin Water	Yang Water	Yin Metal	Yang Metal	Yin Earth	Yang Earth
Branch	Horse	Snake	Dragon	Rabbit	Tiger	Ox	Rat	Pig	Dog
Main Element	Yin Fire	Yang Fire	Yang Earth	Yin Wood	Yang Wood	Yin Earth	Yin Water	Yang Water	Yang Earth
Hidden Elements	Yin Earth	Yang Earth Yang Metal	Yin Wood Yin Water		Yang Fire Yang Earth	Yin Water Yin Metal		Yang Water Yang Wood	Yin Metal Yin Fire

Element	Organ	Relative Strength	Total Element	Percentage	Condition
Water	Kidney	50	50	9%	Weak
Wood	Liver	100	100	19%	Balanced
Fire	Small Intestine Heart	100 170	270	50%	Excess
Earth	Spleen	15	15	3%	Weak
Metal	Lung	100	100	19%	Balanced

Day Stem is Water.

Strengthening elements: Metal-parent (100) and Water-sibling (0) = 100

Weakening elements: Wood (100), Fire (270), Earth (15) = 385

This is a weak Water Day Stem.

Being weak Water, illnesses tend to be chronic. It is important to resolve any illnesses quickly, preventing the opportunity for the illness to develop and become chronic. It is very important to balance the Four Pillar condition, in this case this person is very susceptible to developing chronic Fire, Earth and Metal conditions.

Fire is very strong and its influence on Metal is very unfavorable. Special focus must be used to balance this condition. This is an example of a very strong element controlling and negatively influencing another element.

1. Ten-Year Life cycle 38 is Yang Water and it combines with the Four Pillar Year Stem Yin Fire, they have the potential to transform into Wood. There is no Root in the Month Branch, therefore no transformation occurs.

2. The Month Stem in the Four Pillars is Yang Fire and it combines with the Yin Metal Stem in the 10-Year Life cycle, Age 48, they have the potential to transform into Water. There is no Root in the Month Branch, therefore no transformation occurs.

3. The Month Stem Yang Earth in the 10-Year Life cycle age 78 combines with the Yin Water in the Day Stem to potentially transform into Fire. There is Root in the Month Branch. There is no Controller of Fire, which is Water in the Four Pillars and there is additional Fire supporting this transformation. The Transformation occurs.

Chapter 13

Five Element Correspondences

The following section includes general attributes for each of the Five Elements. A Four Pillars chart contains a blend of Five Elements; the key is learning how to determine the condition of the Four Pillars, especially how specific qualities will be expressed. The Day Stem represents the Self or the person. It is the predominant element in the Four Pillars, how other elements influence it must be evaluated. For example, Fire represents charisma, energy and leadership. A weak Fire person under great stress from its controlling element may express their Fire nature with frustration, impulsiveness and aggression.

Water

Water can nourish or deteriorate. Water people communicate well, are gentle, caring and are susceptible to fear. They are not straightforward; they prefer a soft, gentle and indirect way of interaction. Water people are good at both sides of communication, listening and talking. They use their emotional sensitivity to influence people and can be greatly influenced by others and their environment. Water people unify others with emotional energy and understanding. They trust their intuition and use flexibility and perseverance to succeed.

Element	Water
Movement	Adaptable, Flexible
Season	Winter
Direction	North
Planet	Mercury
Color	Blue, Black
Compatible Profession	Teaching, communication, transportation, fishing, divination, lecturing, healers.
Relationships	Water is the sibling. Wood is the child. Fire is the grandchild. Earth is the grandparent. Metal is the parent.
Organs	Kidneys – Rat Urinary Bladder—Pig
Emotions	Gentleness Fear
Sense Orifice	Hearing
Tissues	Bones
Taste	Salty
Spirit	Zhi – Will Power

Wood

Wood represents growth. It is expansive and provides direction to achieving goals. Wood people can turn resources into products, ideas into profits, and believe expansion or growth will resolve any problems. Wood people are very sociable and are almost always surrounded by others; they have good verbal skills. Woods are extroverted and love to accomplish or complete activities.

Wood people can have strong tempers and feel frustrated when other people fail to perform to their standards. They can be scattered, spreading themselves and their resources too thin. Wood types may find it difficult to express their inner emotions, have few close friends and can suffer from feeling inadequate. They can handle great amounts of pressure. Wood types are practical people who are always looking to the future.

Element	Wood
Movement	Growth, Ascension.
Season	Spring
Direction	East
Planet	Jupiter
Color	Green
Compatible Profession	Education, writing, publishing, apparel manufacturing, fashion, herbal products, wood related industries.
Relationships	Water is the sibling. Wood is sibling. Fire is child. Earth is grandchild. Metal is grandparent.
Organs	Liver – Rabbit Gallbladder – Tiger
Sense	Vision
Taste	Sour
Tissues	Tendons
Emotions	Kindness Anger
Spirit	Hun – Direction, Planning

Fire

Fire warms, clarifies and comforts, but can also burn and destroy. It can illuminate or bring light to a situation, or can create explosive actions. Fire people are leaders, motivators and take-charge people. They are highly charismatic, very self-driven, and passionate. If nothing is going on, they will ignite a spark to create something. They are adventurous and are always looking for something new. Change is a predominant theme for them, and they often leap before looking. This can create great successes and great problems. Fire people want to be the center of attention.

Fire people are good speakers, but can be poor listeners. They are creators and think and act fast. They are brave, take on all challenges, and are good warriors. Fire people can be flamboyant, filled with passion, and make life exciting. They need to keep their excitement, passion and enthusiasm in balance and develop patience.

Element	Fire
Movement	Active, vitality.
Season	Summer
Direction	South
Planet	Mars
Color	Red
Compatible Profession	Restaurant, alcohol, electricity, entertainment, power sources.
Relationships	Wood is the parent. Fire is sibling. Earth is the child. Metal is the grandchild. Water is the grandparent.
Organs	Heart—Horse Small Intestine – Snake
Sense	Taste
Taste	Bitter
Tissues	Blood Vessels
Emotions	Joy, Love Hastiness, Impatience, Hatred
Spirit	Shen — represents all aspects of Spirit

Earth

Earth provides stability and is a transformer. In the Five Elements, it is the transforming energy from one season to another or from one element to another. Fairness is often a predominant quality in an Earth person and they tend to be chronic worriers, in fact they may worry about everything, not only their direct life, but everything in the universe. They are steady and do not move as fast as others, but what they lack in speed, they make up with consistency and longevity. They do not like to waste their time in grand schemes or ideas; instead, they plow through the realities of a situation.

Earth people make wonderful managers or organizers; they can be trusted with implementing a plan. However, their focus, practicality and perseverance may result in a single-mindeness, which hinders versatility and the ability to handle multiple factors simultaneously. Earth people are not overly emotional, but are sensitive. They resolve emotional problems in practical, concrete ways. Earth people expect the rest of the world to view life as they do, if they do not, Earth types can become stubborn and rigid. They respond well to change, if the change is slow and gradual, abrupt changes disturb them.

Element	Earth
Movement	Stability, stillness.
Season	Indian Summer.
Direction	North East, South West, Center
Planet	Saturn
Color	Yellow, beige.
Compatible Profession	Construction, real estate, attorney, judges, human resources, management, consultation.
Relationships	Fire is the parent. Earth is the sibling. Metal is the child. Water is the grandchild. Wood is the grandparent.
Tissues	Flesh
Organs	Spleen – Ox, Sheep Stomach – Dragon, Dog
Emotions	Openness, Fairness Worry
Spirit	Yi—Concentration

Metal

etal can be a precious substance, for example, Gold, or a destructive device, a sword. Metal communicates information; it can relay information smoothly. Metal people can gather others for positive goals or negative objectives. They can be focused, emotional, intuitive, confident and aggressive in pursuing goals. Metals tend to be loners, isolated and often withdraw. Metal types may be stubborn, driven by an inner faith whether they are right or wrong. They can be extremely driven to pursue their goals. When problems arise, they will turn inward to find answers, and cannot be expected to communicate their inner feelings. Metals can be successful in any profession, and can also motivate others to achieve common objectives.

Metals can be susceptible to sadness, which can dominate their life. If they become more flexible and open, they will develop loyal friendships. Metal represents righteousness, justice and truth, as well as, sadness, grief, and longing.

Element	Metal
Movement	Inward
Season	Fall
Direction	West, North West
Planet	Venus
Color	White, Gold
Compatible Profession	Metal related industries, strategic management, automobile industry and jewelry.
Relationships	Water is the child. Wood is the grandchild. Fire is the grandparent. Earth is the parent. Metal is the sibling.
Tissues	Flesh
Organ	Lungs – Cock Large Intestine – Monkey
Emotions	Courage Sadness, Depression
Spirit	Po – Corporeal Soul

Five Element Relationships

Once the relative strength of each element is determined and favorable and unfavorable elements are identified, universal Five Element relationships can be applied to enhance the quality of life. For instance, a weak Water person can design their wardrobe and living environment with beneficial elements, directions, colors and gemstones. The information in Tables 13a-b can be applied to one's life based on their Four Pillars. These applications are examples of the integration of Heaven, Man and Earth.

Table 13a

Five Element Relationship Chart

Element	Color Primary	Color Secondary	Direction	Organs	Gemstones	Planet
Wood	Green	Blue	East South East	Liver Gallbladder	Emerald, Jade, Green Opal	Jupiter
Fire	Red	Purple, Pink	South	Heart Small Intestine Pericardium San Jiao	Red Ruby	Mars
Earth	Yellow	Beige, Brown	North East South West Center	Spleen Stomach	Yellow Opal, Yellow Diamond	Saturn
Metal	White Gold	Silver Shiny	North West West	Lungs Large Intestine	Pearl, Crystal, White Diamond	Venus
Water	Blue Black	Grey	North	Kidneys Urinary Bladder	White Opal, Blue Sapphire	Mercury

Table 13b

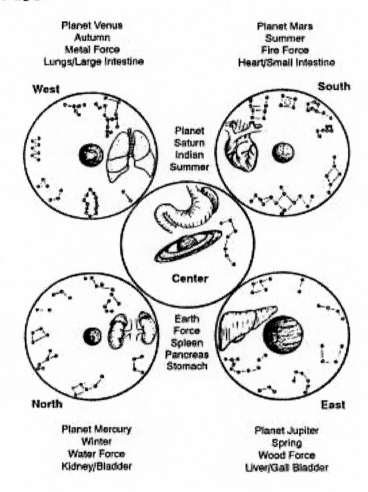

Planet Venus
Autumn
Metal Force
Lungs/Large Intestine

Planet Mars
Summer
Fire Force
Heart/Small Intestine

West

South

Planet
Saturn
Indian
Summer

Center

Earth
Force
Spleen
Pancreas
Stomach

North

East

Planet Mercury
Winter
Water Force
Kidney/Bladder

Planet Jupiter
Spring
Wood Force
Liver/Gall Bladder

Chapter 14

General Principles for Health

A profound principle in Oriental Medicine is balance. An element or organ is healthy when balanced. In the Four Pillars *adjacent elements have a strong influence on an element, it can make the element strong, weak or in harmony. No formula can calculate this influence. Experience will develop this skill.* The following are general principles for evaluating a Four Pillars chart.

- When an element is not present in the Four Pillars the related organ is weak or is susceptible to disorders.
- When an element is controlled by a strong element it is very susceptible to disorders. When the controlling cycle causes a health problem, the process is referred to as overacting. Generally, overacting leads to unfavorable health.
- If the Day Stem is weak the illnesses tend to be of a chronic nature and take time to cure. Chapter 10 explains calculating the condition of the Day Stem.
- If the Day Stem is strong the illnesses tend to be acute and take a short time to cure. Chapter 10 explains calculating the condition of the Day Stem.
- If the element causing the illness is weak the illness is not strong.
- If the element causing the illness is strong the illness is strong.

- The parent element will increase the strength and influence of its child element when the child is excessive. If the parent is controlled by its grandparent, the parent's influence on the excessive element is weakened.

- Day, Month, Year and 10-Year Life cycles must be evaluated to predict how nature's energetic cycles affect the Four Pillars and health. This is one aspect of the influences of time.

Example

Male born on June 30, 1957 at 6:30 am, day light saving time.

Four Pillars

	Hour	Day	Month	Year
Stem	Yin Wood Liver 100X 50%	Yin Water Kidney 100 X 50%	Yang Fire Small Intestine 100 X 100%	Yin Fire Heart 100 X 100%
Branch	Rabbit	Cock	Horse	Cock
Elements	Yin Wood Liver 100 X 50%	Yin Metal Lung 100 X 50%	Yin Fire Heart 70 X 100% Yin Earth Spleen 30 X 50%	Yin Metal Lung 100 X 50%

Element	Organ	Relative Strength	Total Element	Percentage	Condition
Water	Kidney	50	50	9%	Weak
Wood	Liver	100	100	19%	Balanced
Fire	Small Intestine Heart	100 170	270	50%	Excess
Earth	Spleen	15	15	3%	Weak
Metal	Lung	100	100	19%	Balanced

Analysis

- Excess Fire
- Deficient Earth
- Fire overacts on Metal creating potential Lung and Large Intestine conditions.
- The deficient Earth receives some energy from its resource Fire. Fire promotes or supplements Earth. The Earth is weak, this makes the person susceptible to Earth disorders.
- The deficient Earth falls to nourish Metal contributing to Metal disharmonies.
- Deficient Water obtains some energy from its resource Metal.

Objective

- Clear excess Fire from Heart and Small Intestine.
- Clear Fire from Metal organs, Lung and Large Intestine.
- Supplement Earth, Metal and Water or the Spleen, Stomach, Lung, Large Intestine, Kidney and Urinary Bladder.

Day Stem is Water.

Strengthening elements: Metal-parent (100) and Water-same (0)=100

Weakening elements: Wood (100), Fire (270), Earth (15)=385

This is a weak Water Day Stem.

Being weak Water, illnesses tend to be chronic. It is important to resolve any illnesses quickly, preventing the opportunity for the illness to develop and become chronic. It is very important to balance the Four Pillar condition, in this case this person is very susceptible to developing chronic Fire, Earth and Metal conditions.

Fire is very strong and its influence on Metal is very unfavorable. Special focus must be used to balance this condition. This is an example of a very strong element controlling and negatively influencing another element.

Chapter 15

Five Element-Organ Syndromes

Table 15a lists basic conditions for each of the internal organs. Example 15b applies Five Element symptoms to a Four Pillar birth chart.

Table 15a

Element	Organ	Excess	Deficiency
Water	Kidney	No Excess Conditions	Dizziness, tinnitus, vertigo, deafness, poor memory, thirst, sore back, knee pain, night sweats, red cheek bones, insomnia, hyper-sexual activity, constipation. Fatigue, frequent urination, diarrhea, cold limbs and back, pale face, impotence, premature ejaculation, edema of legs, infertility, loose stools, incontinence, spermatorrhea, shortness of breath, difficulty inhaling, cough, asthma. Poor bone development, softening of bones, loose teeth, premature graying of hair, lacks of sexual energy.
	Urinary Bladder	Frequent, burning or difficult urination, dark-yellow or turbid urination, fever, thirst, copious and clear urine.	Frequent, pale urination, incontinence, enuresis.
Wood	Liver	Distention or pain of the hypochondria and chest, sighing, hiccup, fluctuation of mental and emotional state, nausea, vomiting, poor appetite, a feeling of a lump in throat, irritability, anger, menstrual disorders, PMS, headache, digestive disorders, dizziness, convulsions, tremor of limbs, numbness of limbs, bitter taste, jaundice, vaginal discharge and itching,	Anemia, menstrual disorders, numbness of limbs, weak nails, dizziness, blurred vision, menstrual irregularities, pale expressions, pale lips, muscular weakness, muscle spasms, cramps, brittle nails,
	Gallbladder	Hypochondriac pain, nausea, vomiting, inability to digest fats, yellow complexion, and bitter taste.	Dizziness, blurred vision, nervousness, timidity, lack of courage, sighing.

Table 15a

Element	Organ	Excess	Deficiency
Fire	Heart	Palpitations, thirst, mouth and tongue ulcers, mental restlessness, heat, insomnia, red face, bitter taste, dream disturbed sleep, incoherent speech, pain in the heart region which can radiate to inner aspect of the left arm, feeling of oppression of chest.	Palpitations, shortness of breath on exertion, sweating, pallor, fatigue, listlessness, dizziness, insomnia, dream-disturbed sleep, poor memory, malar flushed face, low grade fever, feeling of heat
	Small Intestine	Mental restlessness, tongue ulcers, pain in throat, abdominal pain, thirst, scanty and dark urine, painful urination, blood in urine. Lower abdominal twisting pain which may radiate to the back, abdominal distention, borborygmus, flatulence, pain in testis, dislike of abdominal pressure, constipation, vomiting, diarrhea.	Abdominal discomfort, borborygmus, Scanty urination, flatulence, and diarrhea.
Earth	Spleen	Lack of Appetite, stuffiness of epigastrium, feeling of cold, heaviness sensation of the head, sweetish taste, loose stools, fatigue, feeling of heaviness of the body, thirst without a desire to drink, nausea, vomiting, burning sensation of the anus, edema.	Lack of appetite, abdominal distention after eating, fatigue, sallow complexion, weakness of limbs, loose stools, shortness of breath, nausea, feeling of heaviness, chilliness, cold limbs, prolapsed of stomach, uterus, anus or vagina, blood spots under the skin, blood in the urine or stools, menorrhagia, vericose veins, edema.
	Stomach	Burning sensation in the epigastrium, thirst for cold liquids, constant hunger, swelling, pain or bleeding gums, nausea, vomiting after eating, bad breath. Sudden pain in the epigastrium, feeling of cold, vomiting of clear fluid.	Lack of appetite, loose stools, fatigue, weak limbs, discomfort epigastrium, nausea, belching, vomiting, hiccup. Fever or feeling of heat in the afternoon, constipation, epigastric pain, dry mouth and throat, feeling of fullness after eating.
Metal	Lung	Chronic cough, phlegm-clear or yellow, stuffiness of chest, shortness of breath, asthma.	Shortness of breath, cough, weak voice, catches colds easily, fatigue, dry throat, low-grade fever, night sweating, thirst.
	Large Intestine	Abdominal pain, diarrhea, mucous in blood, burning anus, smelly stools, fever, sweating, scanty dark urine, constipation, cold, diarrhea with pain, chronic diarrhea, prolapsed anus, hemorrhoids, cold limbs, borborygmus.	Diarrhea, constipation, prolapsed anus, hemorrhoids, abdominal distention.

When a color is predominant on the body it is often an indicator of a disharmony with the corresponding organ system. For example, if someone has a red face and eyes it may reflect excess Fire. If the lower eyelids were a dark shade, it may reflect a Water or Kidney disharmony. Connect the predominant color to the Organ-Element system and refer to the Five Element-Organ System table to identify possible syndromes. If the syndromes, color and element match, this confirms the organ is out of balance. Use the harmonizing techniques in Chapters 16-21 to find balance and health.

Example 15b

Four Pillars

	Hour	Day	Month	Year
Stem	Yin Wood Liver 100X 50%	Yin Water Kidney 100 X 50%	Yang Fire Small Intestine 100 X 100%	Yin Fire Heart 100 X 100%
Branch Elements	Rabbit Yin Wood Liver 100 X 50%	Cock Yin Metal Lung 100 X 50%	Horse Yin Fire Heart 70 X 100% Yin Earth Spleen 30 X 50%	Cock Yin Metal Lung 100 X 50%

Element	Organ	Relative Strength	Total Element	Percentage	Condition
Water	Kidney	50	50	9%	Weak
Wood	Liver	100	100	19%	Balanced
Fire	Small Intestine Heart	100 170	270	50%	Excess
Earth	Spleen	15	15	3%	Weak
Metal	Lung	100	100	19%	Balanced

Analysis

- **Excess Fire**
  Palpitations, thirst, mouth and tongue ulcers, mental restlessness, heat, insomnia, red face, bitter taste, dream disturbed sleep, incoherent speech, pain in the heart region which can radiate to inner aspect of the left arm, feeling of oppression of chest.

- **Deficient Earth**
  Lack of appetite, abdominal distention after eating, fatigue, sallow complexion, weakness of limbs, loose stools, shortness of breath, nausea, feeling of heaviness, chilliness, cold limbs, prolapse of stomach,

uterus, anus or vagina, blood spots under the skin, blood in the urine or stools, menorrhagia, vericose veins.

Lack of appetite, loose stools, fatigue, weak limbs, discomfort epigastrium, nausea, belching, vomiting, hiccup. Fever or feeling of heat in the afternoon, constipation, epigastric pain, dry mouth and throat, feeling of fullness after eating.

- **Excess Fire overacts on Metal, creating potential Lung and Large Intestine syndromes. This is the most predominant constitutional condition.**

  Chronic cough, phlegm-clear or yellow, stuffiness of chest, shortness of breath, asthma, weak voice, catches colds easily, fatigue, dry throat, low-grade fever, night sweating, thirst, diarrhea, constipation, prolapsed anus, hemorrhoids, abdominal distention

- **The deficient Earth receives some energy from its resource Fire. Fire promotes or supplements Earth. There is a high potential for digestive difficulties.**

- **The deficient Earth falls to nourish Metal contributing to Metal disharmonies.**

- **Water deficiency**

  Dizziness, tinnitus, vertigo, deafness, poor memory, thirst, sore back, knee pain, night sweats, red cheek bones, insomnia, hypersexual activity, constipation.

Excess Fire dries up and weakens Water. Water normally controls Fire but in this case Fire is so strong it negatively effects Water. This is commonly referred to as the Insulting cycle, it is when the controlled element is so strong or there is a strong imbalance, it attacks and negatively influences the controlling element.

Chapter 16

Natural Harmonizing Techniques

Acupuncture Points

This chapter introduces a variety of basic practices and techniques to enhance health. These natural practices include utilization of traditional Acupuncture points, Qi Gong, Five Element Cosmology and influences of the Seasons. Foods and Herbs can also used. Table 16a lists Acupuncture points for each element and their corresponding organ. Acupuncture points are listed for excess and deficient conditions. Refer to the Appendix for recommended readings.

Table 16a

Element	Organ	Excess	Deficiency
Water	Kidney		Kidney 3, 6, 7 Bladder 23 Ren 4 Spleen 6 Five Element Treatment: Kidney 7
	Urinary Bladder	Bladder 28, 40, 58, 60, 62, 64 Five Element Treatment: Bladder 65	Bladder 23, 40, 60, 62 Kidney 3, 6, 7 Ren 3 Five Element Treatment: Bladder 67
Wood	Liver	Liver 2, 3, 5, 14 Pericardium 6 Bladder 18 Five Element Treatment: Liver 2	Liver 3, 5, 8. 14 Bladder 18 Liver 8
	Gallbladder	Gallbladder 20, 24, 30, 31, 34, 40, 41 Bladder 19 Five Element Treatment: Bladder 65	Gallbladder 20, 30, 31, 34, 41 Bladder 19 Five Element Treatment: Bladder 67
Fire	Heart	Heart 3, 6, 7, 8 Ren 14, 17 Pericardium 6 Bladder 14, 15 Five Element Treatment: Heart 7	Heart 1, 3, 7 Ren 14, 17 Pericardium 6 Bladder 14, 15 Five Element Treatment: Heart 9
	Small Intestine	Small Intestine 3, 6, 7 Ren 4 Bladder 27 Five Element Treatment: Small Intestine 8	Small Intestine 3, 7 Ren 4 Bladder 27 Five Element Treatment: Small Intestine 3
Earth	Spleen	Spleen 4, 6, 9, 10 Ren 4, 12 Bladder 20, 21 Five Element Treatment: Spleen 5	Spleen 3, 4, 6, 9, 10 Ren 4, 12 Stomach 36 Bladder 20, 21 Five Element Treatment: Spleen 2
	Stomach	Stomach 21, 34, 36, 42, 44 Ren 12 Bladdder 21 Five Element Treatment: Stomach 45	Stomach 21, 36 Ren 12 Spleen 6 Bladder 21 Five Element Treatment: Stomach 41
Metal	Lung	Lung 1, 5, 6, 7, 10 Ren 17 Bladder 13 Five Element Treatment: Lung 5	Lung 1, 7, 9 Ren 17 Bladder 13 Five Element Treatment: Lung 9
	Large Intestine	Large Intestine 4, 6, 11, 15 Stomach 25, 37 Ren 12 Bladder 25 San Jiao 6 Kidney 6 Five Element Treatment: Large Intestine 2	Large Intestine 4, 10 Stomach 25, 37 Ren 12 Bladder 25 Five Element Treatment: Large Intestine 11

Qi Gong

Qi Gong is a major branch of Oriental Medicine and is practiced by millions of people across the world. Qi Gong means energy cultivation or energy exercises. They are gentle movement exercises and breathing techniques that have been used for thousands of years throughout the Orient. The principles of the Five Elements and their corresponding relationships are an integral aspect of Qi Gong. Four Pillars reveals the constitutional Five Elements condition of a person and Qi Gong is a method to find balance and harmony among the Five Elements-Organs. Qi Gong practices are particularly effective in balancing stress and negative emotions. Each organ has a positive and negative set of emotions. Stress and negative emotions can influence organ functions, drain energy and contribute to many diseases. In most systems of self-development balancing or harmonizing emotions is the initial goal. It is also the foundation for health and vitality. Figure 16a illustrates each organ and the unfavorable effects negative emotions exert.

Figure 16a

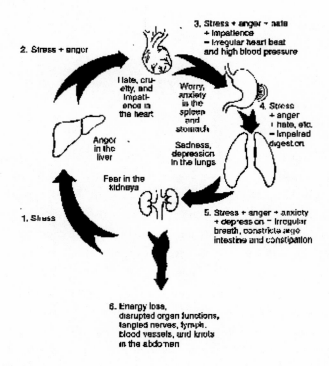

Table 16b lists major Five Elements relationships for Qi Gong. Two major Qi Gong practices for harmonizing stress and emotions are Five Element Healing Sounds and the Five Element Smile.

Table 16b

Element	Organ	Color	Sound	Emotions
Water	Kidney	Blue	Woooo	Gentleness
	Bladder	Black	Like blowing out a candle	Fear
Wood	Liver	Green	Shhhh	Kindness
	Gallbladder		Like Shhhhhhing a little child	Anger
Fire	Heart	Red	Haw	Joy, Love
	Small Intestine			Hastiness, Hate
Earth	Spleen	Yellow	Whooo	Openness
	Stomach		The sound comes from the throat.	Worry
Metal	Lung	White	SSSSS	Courage
	Large Intestine			Sadness, Depression

The Five Element Healing Sounds
Diagram 16b

1. Begin by sitting naturally in a chair, open your eyes and place your mind's attention in the Lungs. Take a slow, full, inhale, breathing into the abdomen.
2. Think of sadness and depression, take one long exhale while making the SSSSSSSSSSSSSSSS sound and release sadness and depression during the exhale.
3. Close your eyes, place your hands face up on your thighs, smile while focusing your mind's attention into the white lungs and repeat courage to your self. Do this for 30-60 seconds.
4. Perform steps 1-3, three times.
5. Open your eyes and place your mind's attention in the Kidneys, take a full inhale.
6. Think of fear and take one long exhale while making the Whooooo sound, release fear during the exhale.
7. Close your attention, place your hands face up on your thighs, smile while focusing your mind's eye into the blue-black kidneys and repeat gentleness to your self. Do this for 30-60 seconds.
8. Repeat steps 5-7 from 3 times.
9. Repeat this procedure for the Liver, Heart and Spleen. Do the sounds in the exact order listed.

Diagram 16b
The Five Element Sounds

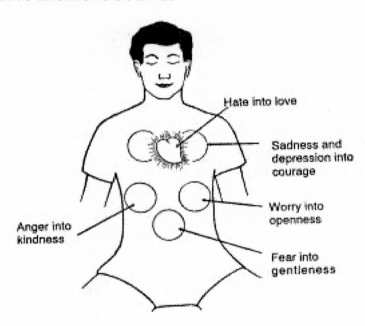

The Five Element Smile
See diagram 16b

1. Smile and place you mind's attention in the red Heart and repeat the words Joy and Love. Feel the emotions in the Heart. Do this for one to three minutes.
2. Move your attention into the white Lungs, Smile and repeat the word courage. Feel the emotion in the Lungs. Do this for one to three minutes.
3. Move your attention to the green Liver, Smile and repeat the word kindness. Feel the emotion in the Liver. Do this for one to three minutes.
4. Move your attention to the yellow Spleen, Smile and repeat the word openness. Feel the emotion in the Spleen. Do this for one to three minutes.
5. Move you attention to the blue-black kidneys, Smile and repeat the word gentleness. Feel the emotion in the Kidneys. Do this for one to three minutes.
6. Move your attention behind the navel and concentrate your attention there for three to five minutes.

Gently open your eyes, stretch and enjoy.

- In general do all Five Element Healing Sounds and complete the Five Element Smile; this will harmonize all organs.
- If an organ is out of balance spend more time on that organ.
- If an organ is in excess, perform the *sound* for that organ 6-12 times.
- If an organ is deficient, spend more time on that organ during the Five Element Smile.

Diagram 16
The Five Element Smile

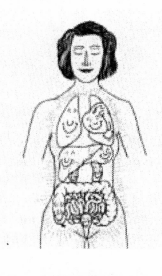

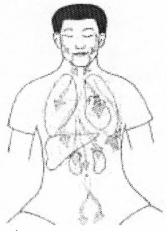

Five Element Cosmology

Five Element cosmology relates the Five Elements to space or direction. Each direction relates to an element, by positioning oneself in specific geographical locations a person can absorb or bathe in the influence of an element. Table 16c lists the Five Elements and directional relationships.

Table 16c

Element	Direction	Element
Water	North	Water Fountain, Aquarium
Wood	East, South East	Plants
Fire	South	Red Candle, Red Items
Earth	South West, North East, Center	Ceramic, Porcelain, Crystals, Soil-based items
Metal	West, North West	Metal clocks, grandfather clocks, Metal items

Use this information to position a person in their favorable directions. Additionally, favorable elements can be added to locations in a home or office to optimize the effects. Feng Shui is the art of living in harmony with one's environment. It is a very deep art with profound influences. The space-location information listed is the most basic aspects of Feng Shui. To learn beginning and advanced levels of Feng Shui refer to my book "Flying Star" Feng Shui Made Easy.

Seasons

E ach element corresponds to a season. The element for a particular season is the predominant force during its cycle. This elemental force can be favorable or unfavorable to a person; it will depend on the Four Pillars condition. The application of this knowledge is to predict how each season will affect a person's health and which techniques can be used to find balance during each season. Table 16d lists the element for each season and Example 16e illustrates how to use the seasonal influences with the Four Pillars.

Table 16d

Season	Element
Winter	Water
Spring	Wood
Summer	Fire
Indian Summer	Earth
Fall	Metal

Example 16e

Four Pillars

	Hour	Day	Month	Year
Stem	Yin Wood Liver 100X 50%	Yin Water Kidney 100 X 50%	Yang Fire Small Intestine 100 X 100%	Yin Fire Heart 100 X 100%
Branch Elements	Rabbit Yin Wood Liver 100 X 50%	Cock Yin Metal Lung 100 X 50%	Horse Yin Fire Heart 70 X 100% Yin Earth Spleen 30 X 50%	Cock Yin Metal Lung 100 X 50%

Element	Organ	Relative Strength	Total Element	Percentage	Condition
Water	Kidney	50	50	9%	Weak
Wood	Liver	100	100	19%	Balanced
Fire	Small Intestine	100	270	50%	Excess
	Heart	170			
Earth	Spleen	15	15	3%	Weak
Metal	Lung	100	100	19%	Balanced

Analysis

- Excess Fire
- Deficient Earth
- Fire overacts on Metal creating potential Lung and Large Intestine syndromes.
- The deficient Earth receives some energy from its resource Fire. Fire promotes or supplements Earth. The Earth is weak, making this person susceptible to Earth disorders.
- The deficient Earth falls to nourish Metal contributing to Metal disharmonies.
- Deficient Water obtains some energy from its resource Metal.

Objective

- Clear excess Fire from the Heart and Small Intestine.
- Clear Fire from Metal organs, Lung and Large Intestine.
- Supplement Earth, Metal and Water.

Seasonal Analysis

- Spring and Summer will increase the existing excess Fire, special emphasis must be placed on reducing Fire and increasing Metal and Water.
- Indian Summer brings some relief; the Earth element drains or reduces Fire.
- Fall and Winter, which reflect Water and Metal, are the best months for this person. Those months provide natural energies to balance the Five Elements.

Chapter 17

Stem and Branch Influences

Determining the condition of the Five Elements is the key to applying Four Pillars knowledge to Health and their related organs. In general, if a Four Pillars chart receives unfavorable energies, unfavorable health conditions manifest. If the Four Pillars chart receives favorable energies, favorable health conditions result.

For each Hour, Day, Month, Year and 10-Year Life Cycle there is a binomial or Stem and Branch combination. These influences affect the condition of health for every person and are used to predict potential health conditions. The following table summarizes the general ways to interpret Stem and Branch influences.

Stem and Branch	Health Influences
Favorable Stem and Branch	Favorable health influences
Favorable Stem Unfavorable Branch	Unfavorable health influences with periods of favorable health
Unfavorable Stem Favorable Branch	Primarily favorable health with periods of stress
Unfavorable Stem and Branch	Primarily unfavorable health and stress

Evaluate the Stem and Branch of Hours, Days, Months, Years or 10-Year Life Cycles to predict how they may influence health. When Stems and Branches meet, refer to Table 15a for symptoms which may occur. Acupuncture points, Qi Gong, Cosmology and Seasonal influences are used to obtain balance and harmony.

145

Branch Combinations

The following are the most influential Branch to Branch combinations. These combinations are used in two major ways. The first is when combinations appear in the Four Pillars. In this case the influence lasts for a lifetime. The second is when a cycle of time Branch, for instance, 10-Year Life Cycle, Annual, Monthly or a Daily Branch combines with the Four Pillars, in this case the influence lasts for that duration of time. These influences can be favorable or unfavorable to one's Four Pillar chart and health.

The following has two sections, the first describes Branch combinations and the second is a summary table for quick and easy reference.

Horary Elements

These Branches-Animals are located in the same geographical area and share the same element. They support each other's element.

1. Snake and Horse. The South and Fire element.
2. Monkey and Cock. The West and Metal Element.
3. Rat and Pig. The North and Water element.
4. Rabbit and Tiger. The East and Wood element.

The influence can be favorable or unfavorable. If there is an excess condition, a Horary Branch will increase the excess, exacerbating the condition. If there is a deficiency, a Horary Branch will strengthen the condition. This concept is applied to all Branch combinations.

Directional Branch Combinations

Three Branches are located in each of the cardinal geographical directions. They create a strong elemental influence when the meet. The combinations are:

1. Wood: Tiger, Rabbit and Dragon in the East.
2. Fire: Snake, Horse and Sheep in the South.
3. Metal: Monkey. Cock and Dog in the West.
4. Water: Pig, Rat and Ox in the North.

If all three meet a very strong elemental force is created. If two branches meet a strong force is created.

Trinity

Trinity Branches release a strong elemental influence. The Trinity element released can provide favorable or unfavorable influences, it will depend on which elements help or hinder the Four Pillars condition. Trinity relationships are Branches that are four locations from each other. There are four sets of three Branches. The following are Trinity relationships.

Branch Combinations	Releases
Cock-Ox-Snake	Metal
Rat-Dragon-Monkey	Water
Rabbit-Sheep-Pig	Wood
Horse-Dog-Tiger	Fire

If 2 are together a mild force is created.
If 3 are together a strong force is created.

Notice the geographical position of the first animal of each Trinity (Diagram 17a). Each is located in the cardinal or middle location. The second and third animals in a Trinity contain the element of the cardinal animal's element, it is in their Hidden elements. When three Branches of a Trinity combine, it releases the Hidden element and becomes very strong and influential. For example, in the Cock-Snake-Ox combination (diagram 17b), Cock is Metal; therefore, the Cock-Ox-Snake Trinity releases Metal. The release of this influence can occur in the Four Pillars or two may appear in the Four Pillars and one in the 10-Year Life, Annual or Monthly cycles. The Ox and Snake have Metal in their Hidden Elements, these Animals contain the same element. When they meet or combine a very strong elemental force is released.

Diagram 17a

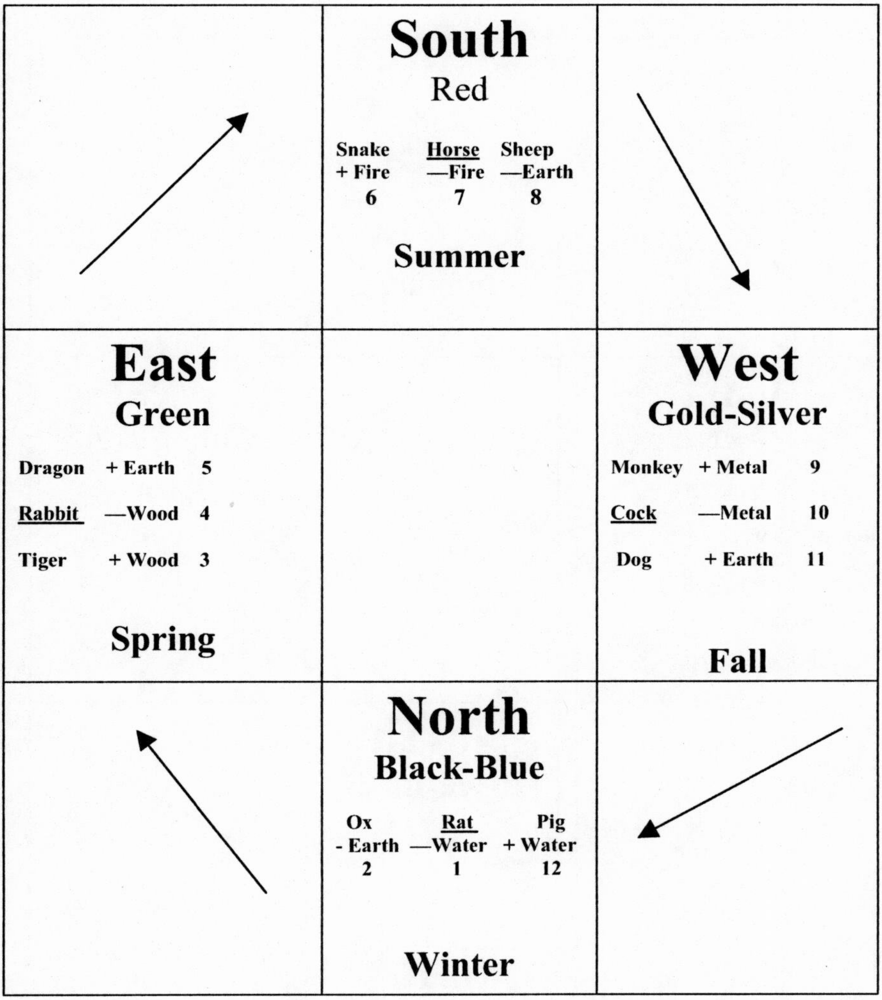

	South Red **Snake** **Horse** **Sheep** + Fire —Fire —Earth 6 7 8 **Summer**	
East Green Dragon + Earth 5 **Rabbit** —Wood 4 Tiger + Wood 3 **Spring**		**West** Gold-Silver Monkey + Metal 9 **Cock** —Metal 10 Dog + Earth 11 **Fall**
	North Black-Blue Ox **Rat** Pig - Earth —Water + Water 2 1 12 **Winter**	

Diagram 17b
Trinity relationships are every fourth Branch or Animal

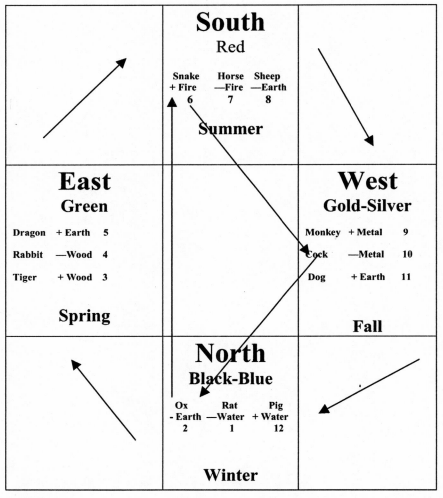

If changes occur because they are triggered by future cycles of time, for example, two Branches are in the Four Pillars and one is in the Annual Branch, an influence may occur which is very strong, for illness, a sudden illness or trauma. This is because a change from one's constitutional condition can be very traumatic. The influence can be favorable or unfavorable depending on the condition of the Four Pillars.

Six Combinations

These Branch combinations pull towards each other and weaken each other's Elemental influence. For example, if the Dragon meets the Rooster, both element's influence is reduced. If the element reduced is favorable to the Four Pillars, an unfavorable health influence will occur. If the element reduced is unfavorable to the Four Pillars, a favorable health influence will occur.

1. Rat and Ox combine.
2. Tiger and Pig combine.
3. Rabbit and Dog combine.
4. Dragon and Cock combine.
5. Snake and Monkey combine.
6. Horse and Sheep combine.

Clash

These combinations cause stress, anxiety and pressure. The branches are in opposite geographical locations. Excluding the Earth element, each combination consists of the controlling cycle. Generally, the controlling element will dominate the other element. If the controlled element is much stronger, it will cause unfavorable influences. If the controlled element is very strong, it will be the predominant force.

1. Rat and Horse. Yin Water and Yin Fire.
2. Ox and Sheep. Earth and Earth.

These Earths enhance the influence it has on the Four Pillars chart. For example, if it is a favorable element, it is enhanced. If it is an unfavorable influence on the Four Pillar chart it is decreased.

3. Tiger and Monkey. Yang Wood and Yang Metal.

4. Rabbit and Cock. Yin Wood and Yin Metal.
5. Dragon and Dog. These two Earths facilitate the influence of their element.
6. Snake and Pig. Yang Fire and Yang Water.

Push Out

These combinations are sometimes called the Four Graves, they include only the four Earth Branches, and cause something to be pushed away or kicked out. It can be favorable or unfavorable; it depends on which element is stronger. The stronger element will kick the other out. Favorable results occur when the negative element in your chart is kicked out and replaced with a beneficial element. Unfavorable results occur when favorable elements are kicked out.

1. Dragon and Dog
2. Sheep and Ox

Conflict

These combinations are part of the Four Graves or Earth Branches. They create stress, pressure and unfavorable influences.

1. Ox and Dog
2. Sheep and Dog

If the Sheep, Dog and Ox combine, there will be a serious obstacle or condition.

Branch Combinations

Branch—Animal	Combination	Meaning
Rat	Pig	Horary Branch
	Ox	Six Combinations
	Horse	Clash
	Pig, Ox	Directional Combination
	Monkey, Dragon	Trinity

Branch—Animal	Combination	Meaning
Ox	Snake, Cock	Trinity
	Sheep	Push Out, Clash
	Dog	Conflict
	Rat	Six Combinations
	Pig, Rat	Directional Combination
	Snake	Push Out

Branch—Animal	Combination	Meaning
Tiger	Rabbit	Horary Branch
	Monkey	Clash
	Pig	Six Combinations
	Rabbit, Dragon	Directional Combination
	Horse, Dog	Trinity

Branch—Animal	Combination	Meaning
Rabbit	Tiger	Horary Branch
	Sheep, Pig	Trinity
	Dog	Six Combinations
	Tiger, Dragon	Directional Combination
	Cock	Clash

Branch—Animal	Combination	Meaning
Dragon	Dog	Push Out, Clash
	Rat, Monkey	Trinity
	Tiger, Rabbit	Directional Combination
	Cock	Six Combinations

Branch—Animal	Combination	Meaning
Snake	Horse	Horary Branch
	Ox, Cock	Trinity
	Monkey	Six Combinations
	Horse, Sheep	Directional Combination
	Pig	Clash

Branch Combinations

Branch—Animal	Combination	Meaning
Horse	Snake	Horary Branch
	Dog, Tiger	Trinity
	Sheep	Six Combinations
	Snake, Sheep	Directional Combination
	Rat	Clash

Sheep	Ox	Push Out, Clash
	Dog	Conflict
	Rabbit, Pig	Trinity
	Horse	'Six Combinations
	Snake, Horse	Directional Combination

Monkey	Cock	Horary Branch
	Tiger	Clash
	Dragon, Rat	Trinity
	Cock, Dog	Directional Combination
	Snake	Six Combinations

Cock	Monkey	Horary Branch
	Rabbit	Clash
	Snake, Ox	Trinity
	Monkey, Dog	Directional Combination
	Dragon	Six Combinations

Dog	Dragon	Push Out, Clash
	Ox	Conflict
	Sheep	Conflict
	Horse, Tiger	Trinity
	Monkey, Cock	Directional Combination
	Rabbit	Six Combinations

Pig	Rat	Horary Branch
	Snake	Clash
	Sheep, Rabbit	Trinity
	Rat, Ox	Directional Combination
	Tiger	Six Combinations

Example

Male born on June 30, 1957 at 6:30 am daylight savings time.

Four Pillars

	Hour	Day	Month	Year
Stem	Yin Wood Liver 100X 50%	Yin Water Kidney 100 X 50%	Yang Fire Small Intestine 100 X 100%	Yin Fire Heart 100 X 100%
Branch **Elements**	Rabbit Yin Wood Liver 100 X 50%	Cock Yin Metal Lung 100 X 50%	Horse Yin Fire Heart 70 X 100% Yin Earth Spleen 30 X 50%	Cock Yin Metal Lung 100 X 50%

Element	Organ	Relative Strength	Total Element	Percentage	Condition
Water	Kidney	50	50	9%	Weak
Wood	Liver	100	100	19%	Balanced
Fire	Small Intestine Heart	100 170	270	50%	Excess
Earth	Spleen	15	15	3%	Weak
Metal	Lung	100	100	19%	Balanced

Analysis

- Excess Fire
- Deficient Earth
- Fire overacts on Metal creating potential Lung and Large Intestine syndromes.
- Deficient Earth receives some energy from its resource Fire. Fire promotes or supplements Earth. The Earth is weak, making the person susceptible to Earth disorders.
- Deficient Earth falls to nourish Metal contributing to Metal disharmonies.
- Deficient Water obtains some energy from its resource Metal.

Branch Combination Analysis

- Rabbit and Cock

  Metal Clashes with Wood. Wood and Metal are balanced in the Four Pillars Chart but Metal controls Wood and the Cock-Metal will pressure the Rabbit-Wood, this will create Liver/Gallbladder disharmonies, particularly anger, frustration and possible a lack of direction in life.

Chapter 18

Cases

The following cases illustrate the procedures and techniques for a Four Pillars health evaluation. Emphasis is placed on the following:

- Calculating the Four Pillars
- Determining the condition of the Five Elements
- Calculating the constitutional condition of the internal organs
- Evaluating Five Element interactions
- Evaluating the influences of future Stem and Branch cycles of time and Seasonal influences
- Applying Five Element harmonizing techniques

The first two cases are comprehensive, select any harmonizing techniques preferred. Cases 3-5 include calculating the Four Pillars, the condition of Five Elements and Internal Organs. Follow the principles of determining the influences of 10-Year Life cycles found in cases 1 and 2. Select one or more harmonizing techniques.

Case 1

Male born on June 30, 1957 at 6:30 am daylight savings time.

Four Pillars

	Hour	Day	Month	Year
Stem	Yin Wood 100 X 50%	Yin Water	Yang Fire 100 X 100%	Yin Fire 100 X 100%
Branch	Rabbit	Cock	Horse	Cock
Elements	Yin Wood 100 X 50%	Yin Metal 100 X 50%	Yin Fire 70 X 100% Yin Earth 30 X 50%	Yin Metal 100 X 50%

10 Year Luck Cycles

Age	0	8	18	28	38	48	58	68	78
Stem	Yang Fire	Yin Wood	Yang Wood	Yin Water	Yang Water	Yin Metal	Yang Metal	Yin Earth	Yang Earth
Branch	Horse	Snake	Dragon	Rabbit	Tiger	Ox	Rat	Pig	Dog
Main Element	Yin Fire	Yang Fire	Yang Earth	Yin Wood	Yang Wood	Yin Earth	Yin Water	Yang Water	Yang Earth
Hidden Elements	Yin Earth	Yang Earth Yang Metal	Yin Wood Yin Water		Yang Fire Yang Earth	Yin Water Yin Metal		Yang Wood	Yin Metal Yin Fire

Element	Organ	Relative Strength	Total Element	Percentage	Condition
Water	Kidney	50	50	9%	Weak
Wood	Liver	100	100	19%	Balanced
Fire	Small Intestine Heart	100 170	270	50%	Excess
Earth	Spleen	15	15	3%	Weak
Metal	Lung	100	100	19%	Balanced

Analysis

- Excess Fire
- Deficient Earth
- Fire overacts on Metal creating potential Lung and Large Intestine syndromes.
- Deficient Earth receives some energy from its resource Fire. Fire promotes or supplements Earth. The Earth is weak, making the person susceptible to Earth disorders.
- Deficient Earth falls to nourish Metal, this contributes to Metal disharmonies.
- Deficient Water obtains some energy from its resource Metal.
- The Day Master is weak Water, this means he is susceptible to chronic illnesses, particularly of the Earth and Metal elements.
- The useful element is Water and the annoying element is Earth. When Earth is excessive, it will dominate Water, causing Water disorders. When this occurs the Kidneys or Urinary Bladder may be intensively influenced.

Four Pillar Branch Combination Analysis

- Rabbit and Cock
  Metal Clashes with Wood. Wood and Metal are balanced in the Four Pillars Chart, but Metal controls Wood and the Cock-Metal will pressure the Rabbit-Wood, this will create Liver/Gallbladder disharmonies, particularly anger, frustration and possible a lack of direction in life.

Ten Year Life Cycles

From 0-7 the Month Pillar is utilized. Yang Fire and Horse provide great pressure, stress and weakness on the Metal element, resulting in Lung and Large Intestine disorders. Fire or the Heart and Small Intestine are very excessive.

Horse and Horse: Horary

Clear Fire heat, nourish Earth and Metal.

From 8-17 there is a Yin Wood Stem and Snake/Fire Branch providing weakness and stress. There is a little Metal in the Hidden Snake element providing some nourishment to the Lungs and Large Intestine. The 10-Year Life cycle Branch Snake and the Four Pillar Horse are good partners, increasing the unfavorable Fire element. The Metal element is unfavorably effected by the Fire element.

Snake and Horse: Horary Elements
Snake and Cock: 2/3rds of Metal Trinity

Clear Fire heat, nourish Earth and Metal.

From 18-27 is Yang Wood and Dragon. Dragon has Yang Earth, Yin Wood and Yin Water elements. The Dragon is also considered wet Earth. Yang Wood is the parent of Fire, it makes it grow. Dragon and Cock are one of the six Combinations. They combine or unite and the Dragon reduces the Metal strength. The Dragon is Earth, which strengthens the Earth element and provides some nourishment to Metal. It also is the child of Fire, thereby reducing. These elements maintain an excessive Fire influence. This person must use techniques to reduce Fire and strengthen Metal. If he does not a chronic and severe Metal condition may have developed.

Dragon and Cock: Six Combinations
Clear Fire and nourish Metal.

From 28-37 there is Yin Water and Rabbit/Yin Wood. The Yin Water controls Fire. The Rabbit is a Clash with the two Cocks and their strength is balanced. The Wood Rabbit is the parent to Fire and provides strength to it. There is a slight Fire increase. Metal must be nourished and Fire reduced.

Rabbit and Cock: Clash

Clear Fire heat and nourish Metal.

From 38-47 the Stem is Yang Water and the Branch is Tiger/Yang Wood. Tiger and Rabbit are Good Partners and increase Wood's strength; it also increases the influence of Fire. The Water Stem controls Fire. The overall effect is Fire is slightly increased.

Tiger and Horse are 2/3rds of Trinity increasing the influence of Fire.

Clear Heart Fire and nourish Meal.

The 48-57 Life Cycle changes to provide the energy and elements needed to contribute towards balance and health. The Stem Yin Metal provides strength to the weak Metal arising from the overacting Fire. The branch Ox is wet Earth, it has the Hidden elements Yin Water and Yin Metal. These Hidden elements provide more strength to Metal. The Hidden Water element controls Fire.

The Cock and Ox are 2/3 of the Metal trinity. It releases some Metal.

From 58-77 favorable influences continue. Yang Metal and Rat/Yin Water provide strength to Metal and Water controls Fire.

Rat and Horse are a Clash. Rat-Water usually wins out but this Four Pillars chart contains excess Fire, the Fire weakens the Rat-Water influence.

Seasonal Influences
Spring nourishes Fire, Clears heat.
Summer intensifies excess Fire, Clears heat.
Indian Summer reduces Fire, weakens Water and supports Earth.
Fall supports Metal and nourishes weak Water.
Winter nourishes weak Water and controls excessive Fire.
Fall and Winter are the most favorable Seasons.

Case 2
Female born on February 18, 1950 at 3:17pm

Four Pillars
Hour Day Month Year Stem

	Hour	Day	Month	Year
Stem	Yang Water 100 X 50%	Yang Wood 100 X 100%	Yang Earth 100 X 50%	Yang Metal 100 X 50%
Branch	Monkey	Monkey	Tiger	Tiger
Elements	Yang Metal 60 X 50%	Yang Metal 60 X 50%	Yang Wood 60 x 100%	Yang Wood 60 x 100%
	Yang Earth 20 x 50%	Yang Earth 20 x 50%	Yang Fire 20 X 80%	Yang Fire 20 X 80%
	Yang Water 20 X 50%	Yang Water 20 X 50%	Yang Earth 20 X 50%	Yang Earth 20 X 50%

10 Year Luck Cycles

Age	5	15	25	35	45	55	65	75
Stem	Yin Fire	Yang Fire	Yin Wood	Yang Wood	Yin Water	Yang Water	Yin Metal	Yang Metal
Branch	Ox	Rat	Pig	Dog	Cock	Monkey	Sheep	Horse
Main Element	Yin Earth	Yin Water	Yang Water	Yang Earth	Yin Metal	Yang Metal	Yin Earth	Yin Fire
Hidden Elements	Yin Water Yin Metal		Yang Wood	Yin Metal Yin Fire		Yang Earth Yang Water	Yin Fire Yin Wood	Yin Earth

Element	Organ	Relative Strength	Total Element	Percentage	Condition
Water	Kidney Urinary Bladder	0 70	70	15%	Balance
Wood	Liver Gallbladder	220	220	47%	Very Excess
Fire	Heart Small Intestine	32	32	7%	Weak
Earth	Spleen Stomach	40	40	8%	Weak
Metal	Lung Large Intestine	110	110	23%	Excess

Analysis

- Very excess Wood
- Excess Metal
- Weak Fire
- Weak Earth
  Water is balanced
- The Day Master is strong Wood, 290 vs 180. This person is susceptible to acute illnesses, particularly effecting the Wood element.
- Wood is very excessive and its controller Metal is strong but not strong enough to control Wood. The predominant situation is excessive Wood disharmonies, including Wood overacting on weak Earth. Earth is very susceptible to being overacted on by Wood.
- Fire is weak but Wood is its parent and it provides some nourishment to strengthen it.

Four Pillar Branch Combination Analysis

- Monkey and Tiger is a Clash. These two Branches are excessive in the Four Pillars chart. Wood, which is the Tiger is very excessive and the predominant element. The Tiger overtakes the Monkey-Metal element. This combination is in the birth chart, which means the Clash actions exist for a lifetime. There will be a lot of stress and difficulties. Because this combination is doubled, the influence is very profound. When the Tiger or Monkey enters during a cycle of time the influence is strong.

Ten Year Life Cycle

From 0-4 the Stem and Branch is Yang Earth and Tiger. The Tiger is primarily Yang Wood adding to the excessive Wood. Yang Earth supports the weak Earth and helps prevent some of the unfavorable influences of Wood overacting on Earth. Excess Wood and deficient Earth are most probable.

Tiger Clashes with two Monkeys in the Four Pillars.

Reduce excess Wood and nourish Earth.

From 5-14 the Stem and Branch is Yin Fire and Ox. Yin Fire nourishes deficient fire and reduces excess Wood. The Ox is Yin Earth, it nourishes deficient Earth, and it has Metal as a Hidden element that helps control excess Wood.

Clear excess Wood

From 15-24 the Stem and Branches are Yang Fire and Rat. Yang Fire nourishes weak Fire, reduces it parent Wood and supports is child weak Earth. Rat is Yin Water, it supports Water and nourishes Wood. The predominant effect is Water nourishes excess Wood.

The Rat and two Monkeys in the Four Pillars make a 2/3 of a Water trinity. Water is strengthened and its nourishing action towards Wood is increased.

Reduce Wood

From 25-34 the Stem and Branch is Yin Wood and Pig. The Stem Yin Wood increases the excess Wood. During this 10 years the person must focus on reducing Wood.

Pig and Tiger are part of the Six Combinations. They combine reducing each other's influence. Wood is so strong the reducing influence is minor.

Reduce Wood

From 35-44 the Stem and Branch is Yang Wood and Dog. Yang Wood strengthens the existing excess Wood. The Dog consists of the main element Earth, it strengthens the weak Earth. The Hidden elements are Fire and Metal. Fire strengthens weak Fire and Metal supports the slightly strong Metal. The Dog combines with the two Monkeys in the Four Pillars, they are 2/3rds of the Metal directional combination. They both are located in the West or Metal element. This combination creates a very strong elemental influence.

Monkey and Dog create a very strong Metal influence which Clashes with the two Tigers in the Four Pillars. This Clash is very potent and can create Wood or Liver-Gallbladder disorders.

Reduce Metal and Wood

From 45-54 the Stem and Branch is Yin Water and Cock. Yin Water nourishes Wood and the Cock strengthens Metal and controls Wood. Cock and two Monkeys from the Four Pillars are 2/3rds of the Metal directional influence. It creates a strong Metal influence. This influence continues the interactions between two excesses Wood and Metal. The Liver-Gallbladder and Lung-Large Intestine are very vulnerable from the stresses of this and the past 10-Year cycle.

Reduce Wood and Metal

From 55-64 the Stem and Branch is Yang Water and Monkey. This continues the pattern of Water and Metal. The Clash is very strong between Metal and Wood.

Monkey and Tiger Clash

Reduce Wood and Metal

From 65-74 the Stem and Branch is Yin Metal and Sheep. Yin Metal strengthens excess Metal and controls Wood. Sheep supports weak Earth. The Hidden Elements of Fire supports weak Fire and Wood strengthens excess Wood.

Reduce Metal and Wood

Seasonal Influences

Spring strengthens excess Wood, reduce Wood.

Summer reduces excess Wood and nourishes weak Fire. Fire controls excess Metal.

Indian Summer supports weak Earth.

Fall supports Metal and nourishes weak Water. Reduce Metal.

Winter supports weak Water and nourishes excess Wood. Reduce Wood.

Summer and Indian Summer are the most favorable seasons.

Case 3

Female born on April 23, 1952 at 4:05pm

Four Pillars

	Hour	Day	Month	Year
Stem	Yang Water 80	Yin Earth 100	Yang Wood 80	Yang Water 80
Branch	Monkey	Pig	Dragon	Dragon
Elements	Yang Metal 30	Yang Water 56	Yang Earth 60	Yang Earth 60
	Yang Earth 20	Yang Wood 24	Yin Wood 16	Yin Wood 16
	Yang Water 16		Yin Water 16	Yin Water 16

10 Year Luck Cycles

Age	0	6	16	26	36	46	56	66
Stem	Yang Wood	Yin Water	Yang Water	Yin Metal	Yang Metal	Yin Earth	Yang Earth	Yin Fire
Branch	Dragon	Rabbit	Tiger	Ox	Rat	Pig	Dog	Cock
Main Element	Yang Earth	Yin Wood	Yang Wood	Yin Earth	Yin Water	Yang Water	Yang Earth	Yin Metal
Hidden Elements	Yin Wood			Yin Water			Yin Metal	
	Yin Water		Yang Fire	Yin Metal		Yang Wood	Yin Fire	
			Yang Earth					

Element	Organ	Relative Strength	Total Element	Percentage	Condition
Water	Kidney Urinary Bladder	32 216	216	37%	Excess
Wood	Liver Gallbladder	32 104	104	18%	Balanced
Fire	Heart Small Intestine	0 0	0	0%	Weak
Earth	Spleen Stomach	100 140	240	40%	Excess
Metal	Lung Large Intestine	0 30	30	5%	Weak

Analysis

- Excess Water
- Excess Earth
- Weak Fire. Fire is completely deficient
- Weak Metal
- The Day Master is slightly weak, 270 vs 320. This patient is susceptible to chronic conditions.
- Monkey and Dragon are 2/3rds of the Water Trinity. The pig is located in the North, which is the Water element. These three Branches create a strong Water influence.
- Reduce Water
- Strengthen Fire
- Strengthen Metal
- Reduce Earth
- Favorable Seasons: Summer, Fall
- Unfavorable Seasons: Winter, Indian Summer

Case 4

Female born on December 18, 1925 at 5:35pm

Four Pillars

	Hour	Day	Month	Year
Stem	Yin Fire 50	Yang Fire 50	Yang Earth 50	Yin Wood 50
Branch	Cock	Rat	Rat	Ox
Elements	Yin Metal 50	Yin Water 100	Yin Water 100	Yin Earth 30 Yin Metal 10 Yin Water 20

10 Year Luck Cycles

Age	0	6	16	26	36	46	56	66	76
Stem	Yang Earth	Yin Earth	Yang Metal	Yin Metal	Yang Water	Yin Water	Yang Wood	Yin Wood	Yang Fire
Branch	Rat	Ox	Tiger	Rabbit	Dragon	Snake	Horse	Sheep	Monkey

Element	Organ	Relative Strength	Total Element	Percentage	Condition
Water	Kidney Urinary Bladder	220 0	220	43%	Excess
Wood	Liver Gallbladder	50 0	50	10%	Weak
Fire	Heart Small Intestine	50 50	100	20%	Balanced
Earth	Spleen Stomach	30 50	80	16%	Slight Weak
Metal	Lung Large Intestine	60 0	60	12%	Weak

Analysis

- Excess Water
- Weak Earth, Slightly Weak Wood
- Metal and Fire are balanced

- The Day Master is weak, 230 vs 380. This person is susceptible to chronic conditions.

- Favorable Seasons: Indian Summer, Spring, Fall, Summer
- Unfavorable Seasons: Winter

- Reduce Water
- Supplement Earth and Wood
- Harmonize Metal and Fire

Case 5

Male born on September 7, 1958 at 12:30pm

Four Pillars

	Hour	Day	Month	Year
Stem	Yang Fire 50	Yin Fire 50	Yang Metal 100	Yang Earth 50
Branch	Horse	Pig	Monkey	Dog
Elements	Yin Fire 35 Yin Earth 15	Yang Water 56 Yang Wood 15	Yang Metal 60 Yang Earth 10 Yang Water 16	Yang Earth 30 Yin Metal 20 Yin Fire 10

10 Year Luck Cycles

Age	0	10	20	30	40	50	60	70
Stem	Yin Metal	Yang Water	Yin Water	Yang Wood	Yin Wood	Yang Fire	Yin Fire	Yang Earth
Branch	Cock	Dog	Pig	Rat	Ox	Tiger	Rabbit	Dragon

Element	Organ	Relative Strength	Total Element	Percentage	Condition
Water	Kidney Urinary Bladder	0 72	72	14%	Weak
Wood	Liver Gallbladder	0 15	15	3%	Very Weak
Fire	Heart Small Intestine	95 50	145	28%	Balanced
Earth	Spleen Stomach	15 90	105	20%	Balanced
Metal	Lung Large Intestine	20 160	180	35%	Excess

Analysis

- Excess Metal
- Very Weak Wood
- Weak Water
- Fire and Earth are balanced
- The Day Master (Yin Fire) is very weak; 150 vs 357. This person is very susceptible to chronic conditions.
- Excess Metal overacting on weak Wood is the predominant disharmony.
- Reduce Metal
- Strengthen Wood, Water and Fire
- Favorable Seasons: Spring, Summer and Winter
- Unfavorable Season: Fall

Chapter 19

Traditional Chronotherapeutic Acupuncture

Traditional Chronotherapeutic Acupuncture is based on the natural cycles of Vital Substances within the body. The general principle of this technique is Vital Substances follow a specific pattern of circulation through Acupuncture channels. The pattern is based on the Meridian clock, this clock measures the Waxing and Waning stages of Vital Substances through a twenty four-hour period. There are a variety of systems in Traditional Chronotherapeutic Acupuncture, some are practical and easily applied in modern society and others are impractical. In this chapter the ancient system of Ling Gui Ba Fa is introduced. It is a highly effective and practical Chronotherapeutic technique.

The essence of Time Acupuncture is identifying the location of Vital Substances during specific times of the day, this allows the practitioner to access and harmonize the Vital Substances to enhance health and vitality. Time Acupuncture includes formulas that identify the time when a specific Acupoint directly connects and influences Vital Substances. It is a catalyst for activating the self-healing mechanisms in the body. An important concept to understand is that the waxing time reveals where and when Vital Substances are full and accessible, by accessing them all parts of the body are influenced. It is a common misunderstanding to think the channel that is waxing is only effected.

The fundamental difference between traditional Acupuncture methods and Time Acupuncture is the types of points selected. Time Acupuncture is based on selecting acupoints during optimal times. *Ling Gui Ba Fa uses the Eight Master Points of the Extraordinary Channels.* This system accesses and activates the body's Vital Substances, not in a limited way, but a macro way. They affect the total Substances in the body and those Substances facilitate obtaining homeostasis and health. *Chronotherapeutic Acupuncture points should be used in conjunction with traditional Acupuncture points. They can be viewed as keys to optimally activating the body's Vital Substances to facilitate a treatment plan.*

Ling Gui Ba Fa

L*ing Gui Ba Fa or The Eight Techniques of the Mysterious Turtle* is an ancient Acupuncture technique for applying Stems, Branches, Eight Trigrams and the Master Points of the Eight Extraordinary Channels. The Eight Extraordinary channels influence the most profound levels of health. The Classic texts state "The 360 Acupuncture points on the twelve regular channels are controlled by the 66 points on the extremities, the 66 points on the extremities are controlled by the 8 Master Points. These Master Points can treat 243 kinds of symptoms and diseases". The Eight Master Points are the key to utilizing the deepest aspects of Oriental Medicine.

According to legend the ancient Chinese sage Fu Xi, saw a magical turtle emerge from the Yellow River. On its back was a pattern of the Eight Trigrams, this pattern is referred to as the River Map, it combines two trigrams in each of the four cardinal directions. See Table 19a.

Table 19a

Fu Xi 's Trigrams

	South Fire 4, 9	
East Wood 3, 8	Center Earth 5, 10	West Metal 2, 7
	North Water 1, 6	

The Nine Palaces or Magic Square are discussed in the "The Scripture of the Luo" and is the basis for Ling Gui Ba Fa. Odd numbers are Yang and represent the Celestial and even numbers are Yin and represent the terrestrial. The numbers in the four directions (South, West, North, East) are odd and relate to the celestial. The numbers in the four corners (South East, South West, North West, North East) are even and relate to the terrestrial.

Table 19b

Post-Heaven Arrangement of Gua

South East Wood 4	South Fire 9	South West Wood 2
Gallbladder 41	Lung 7	Kidney 6
East Wood 3	Center Earth 5	West Metal 7
San Jiao 5	Kidney 6	Small Intestine 3
North East 8	North Water 1	North West Metal 6
Pericardium 6	Bladder 62	Spleen 4

Table 19c lists each Tigram and its respected element, number and Master Point.

Table 19c

Ling Gui Ba Fa Numbers

Number	Trigram	Element	Master Point
1	Kan	Water	Bladder 62
2 5	Kun	Earth	Kidney 6
3	Chen	Wood Thunder	San Jiao 5
4	Sun	Wood Wind	Gallbladder 41
6	Metal	Metal Heaven	Spleen 4
7	Tui	Metal Lake	Small Intestine 6
8	Ken	Earth Mountain	Pericardium 6
9	Li	Fire	Lung 7

The Ling Gui Ba Fa technique consists of a three-step process.

1. Locate the Binomial number for the treatment Day. This is the Day Stem and Branch and is located in the Appendix (years 1920-2010).

2. Table 19e contains the 12 Double Hours along with every combination of Stems and Branches (Binomials).

- Locate the Binomial number for the treatment Day, it is in the top row.
- Locate the treatment Hour in the first column.
- Identify the intersection of the treatment Hour and treatment Day Binomial, this is the Ling Gui Ba Fa number. Refer to Table 19c for the related Master Point.

Master Points of the Eight Extraordinary Channels are grouped in pairs. It is very effective to use the paired Master Point in a treatment; this point is referred to as the Coupled Point. Use the Ling Gui Ba Fa Master Point first, then utilize its paired Point. Table 19d lists the pairings.

Table 19d

Eight Master Point Pairings

Master Point	Coupled Pair
Lung 7	Kidney 6
Small Intestine 3	Bladder 62
Spleen 4	Pericardium 6
San Jiao 5	Gallbladder 41

Master Point	Coupled Pair
Kidney 6	Lung 7
Bladder 62	Small Intestine 3
Pericardium 6	Spleen 4
Gallbladder 41	San Jiao 5

How to use Table 19e:

- Locate the treatment Day Binomial in the top row.
- Locate the treatment Hour in the first column.
- Find the intersection of the Day Binomial and the treatment Hour, this is the Ling Gui Ba Fa number.
- Refer to Table 19c for the Master Point.

Table 19e

Hour	Binomials				Binomials				Binomials				Binomials		
	1	*2*	*3*	*4*	*5*	*6*	*7*	*8*	*9*	*10*	*11*	*12*	*13*	*14*	*15*
11pm-1am	8	5	2	3	5	5	5	1	7	1	2	2	1	5	3
1am-3am	6	3	5	1	3	3	3	4	5	5	9	6	4	3	1
3am-5am	4	1	3	5	6	1	1	2	3	2	7	4	2	1	4
5am-7am	2	4	1	3	4	5	4	6	1	6	5	1	9	5	2
7am-9am	9	2	8	6	2	3	2	4	4	4	3	5	7	2	9
9am-11am	3	6	6	4	9	6	9	2	2	2	6	3	5	6	7
11am-1pm	7	4	6	2	4	4	4	5	6	6	1	1	5	4	2
1pm-3pm	5	2	4	6	7	2	2	3	4	3	8	5	3	2	5
3pm-5pm	3	5	2	4	5	6	5	1	2	1	6	2	1	6	3
5pm-7pm	1	3	9	1	3	4	3	5	5	5	4	6	8	3	1
7pm-9pm	4	1	7	5	1	1	1	3	3	3	7	4	6	1	8
9pm-11pm	2	5	1	3	8	5	8	6	1	1	5	2	9	5	6

Hour	Binomials				Binomials				Binomials				Binomials		
	16	*17*	*18*	*19*	*20*	*21*	*22*	*23*	*24*	*25*	*26*	*27*	*28*	*29*	*30*
11pm-1am	6	8	4	5	2	1	4	4	2	2	2	6	5	8	5
1am-3am	4	6	1	3	6	8	2	7	6	9	6	4	2	6	3
3am-5am	2	4	5	1	3	6	6	5	4	3	4	2	6	4	6
5am-7am	6	7	6	8	1	4	3	3	2	1	2	5	4	2	4
7am-9am	4	5	1	3	5	2	1	1	5	8	6	3	2	5	2
9am-11am	1	3	5	9	3	5	5	8	3	6	3	1	6	3	6
11am-1pm	5	7	2	4	1	9	3	8	1	1	1	5	3	7	4
1pm-3pm	3	5	6	2	4	7	1	6	5	4	5	3	1	5	1
3pm-5pm	1	8	4	9	2	5	4	4	3	2	3	6	5	3	5
5pm-7pm	5	6	2	3	6	3	2	2	6	9	1	4	3	6	3
7pm-9pm	2	4	6	1	4	6	6	9	4	7	4	2	1	4	1
9pm-11pm	6	2	3	8	2	4	4	3	2	5	2	9	4	2	5

Table 19e

Hour	Binomials				Binomials				Binomials				Binomials		
	31	*32*	*33*	*34*	*35*	*36*	*37*	*38*	*39*	*40*	*41*	*42*	*43*	*44*	*45*
11pm-1am	8	5	3	4	5	5	5	1	6	6	2	2	1	5	4
1am-3am	6	3	6	2	3	3	3	4	4	4	9	6	4	3	2
3am-5am	4	1	4	6	6	1	1	2	2	1	7	4	2	1	5
5am-7am	2	4	2	4	4	5	4	6	9	5	5	1	9	5	3
7am-9am	9	2	9	1	2	3	2	4	3	3	3	5	7	2	1
9am-11am	3	6	7	5	9	6	9	2	1	1	6	3	5	6	8
11am-1pm	7	4	7	3	4	4	4	5	5	5	1	1	5	4	3
1pm-3pm	5	2	5	1	7	2	2	3	3	2	8	5	3	2	6
3pm-5pm	3	5	3	5	5	6	5	1	1	6	6	2	1	6	4
5pm-7pm	1	3	1	2	3	4	3	5	4	4	4	6	8	3	2
7pm-9pm	4	1	8	6	1	1	1	3	2	2	7	4	6	1	9
9pm-11pm	2	5	2	4	8	5	8	6	9	8	5	2	9	5	7

	Binomials				Binomials				Binomials				Binomials		
Hour	*46*	*47*	*48*	*49*	*50*	*51*	*52*	*53*	*54*	*55*	*56*	*57*	*58*	*59*	*60*
11pm-1am	1	8	4	5	2	9	3	4	2	2	2	7	6	8	5
1am-3am	5	6	1	3	6	7	1	7	6	9	6	5	3	6	3
3am-5am	3	4	5	1	3	5	5	5	4	3	4	3	1	4	6
5am-7am	1	7	3	8	1	3	2	3	2	1	2	6	5	2	4
7am-9am	5	5	1	2	5	1	6	1	5	8	6	4	3	5	2
9am-11am	2	3	5	9	3	4	4	8	3	6	3	2	1	3	6
11am-1pm	6	7	2	4	1	8	2	8	1	1	1	6	4	7	4
1pm-3pm	4	5	6	2	4	6	6	6	5	4	5	4	2	5	1
3pm-5pm	2	8	4	9	2	4	3	4	3	2	3	7	6	3	5
5pm-7pm	6	6	2	3	6	2	1	2	6	9	1	5	4	6	3
7pm-9pm	3	4	6	1	4	5	5	9	4	7	4	3	2	4	1
9pm-11pm	1	2	3	8	2	8	3	3	2	5	2	1	5	2	5

Examples

Example 1

Treatment Day is March 5, 1987 at 8:30 am

Treatment Day Binomial is 50, Yin Water, Ox
Treatment Hour is 8:30am
Table 19e: 8:30 am and Day Binomial contains #5
Table 19c: #5 is Kidney 6, the Coupled Master Point is Lung 7

Example 2

Treatment Day is April 8, 1985 at Noon.

Treatment Day Binomial is 14, Yin Fire, Ox
Treatment Hour is Noon
Table 19e: Noon and Day Binomial contains #4
Table 19d: #4 is Gallbladder 41, the Coupled Master Point is San Jiao 5

Appendix

Chinese Calendar
Made Easy ©
Years 1920-2010

by

David Twicken, Ph.D., L.Ac.

1920

	Month		Year				
Find your Day Here	Stem	Branch	Stem	Branch	Day	Day	Time
February 5 – 29,— March 6	Yang Earth	Tiger	Yang Metal	Monkey	Feb	25	4:51
March 6 – April 5	Yin Earth	Rabbit	Yang Metal	Monkey	Mar	54	10:15
April 5 – May 6	Yang Metal	Dragon	Yang Metal	Monkey	April	25	4:12
May 6 – June65	Yin Metal	Snake	Yang Metal	Monkey	May	55	9:03
June 6 – July 7	Yang Water	Horse	Yang Metal	Monkey	June	26	19:19
July 7 – August 8	Yin Water	Sheep	Yang Metal	Monkey	July	56	5:29
August 8– September 8	Yang Wood	Monkey	Yang Metal	Monkey	Aug	27	7:27
September 8 – October 8	Yin Wood	Cock	Yang Metal	Monkey	Sep	58	23:33
October 8 – November 8	Yang Fire	Dog	Yang Metal	Monkey	Oct	28	1:05
November 8 – December 7	Yin Fire	Pig	Yang Metal	Monkey	Nov	59	17:31
December 6 – January 6	Yang Earth	Rat	Yang Metal	Monkey	Dec	29	4:34

1921

	Month		Year				
Find your Day Here	Stem	Branch	Stem	Branch	Day	Day	Time
January 6 – February 4	Yin Earth	Ox	Yang Metal	Monkey	Jan	60	10:05
February 4— March 6	Yang Metal	Tiger	Yin Metal	Cock	Feb	31	16:21
March 6— April 5	Yin Metal	Rabbit	Yin Metal	Cock	Mar	59	10:36
April 5— May 6	Yang Water	Dragon	Yin Metal	Cock	April	30	16:03
May 6– June 6	Yin Water	Snake	Yin Metal	Cock	May	0	10:06
June 6— July 8	Yang Wood	Horse	Yin Metal	Cock	June	31	14:51
July 8— August 8	Yin Wood	Sheep	Yin Metal	Cock	July	1	1:24
August 8— September 8	Yang Fire	Monkey	Yin Metal	Cock	Aug	32	11:17
September 8 – October 9	Yin Fire	Cock	Yin Metal	Cock	Sep	3	14:04
October 9— November 8	Yang Earth	Dog	Yin Metal	Cock	Oct	33	5:22
November 8—December 8	Yin Earth	Pig	Yin Metal	Cock	Nov	4	7:58
December 8 – January 6	Yang Metal	Rat	Yin Metal	Cock	Dec	34	0:07

Branch	Pig	Rat	Ox	Tiger	Rabbit	Dragon	Snake	Horse	Sheep	Monkey	Cock	Dog
Main Element	Yang Water	Yin Water	Yin Earth	Yang Wood	Yin Wood	Yang Earth	Yang Fire	Yin Fire	Yin Earth	Yang Metal	Yin Metal	Yang Earth
Hidden Elements	Yang Wood		Yin Water	Yang Fire		Yin Wood	Yang Earth	Yin Earth	Yang Fire	Yang Earth		Yin Metal
			Yin Metal	Yang Earth		Yin Water	Yang Metal		Yin Wood	Yang Water		Yin Fire

1922

	Month		**Year**				
Find your Day Here	Stem	Branch	Stem	Branch	Day	Day	Time
January 6 – February 4	Yin Metal	Ox	Yin Metal	Cock	Jan	5	10:42
February 4— March 6	Yang Water	Tiger	Yang Water	Dog	Feb	36	22:09
March 6— April 5	Yin Water	Rabbit	Yang Water	Dog	Mar	4	16:25
April 5— May 6	Yang Wood	Dragon	Yang Water	Dog	April	35	21:52
May 6 – June 6	Yin Wood	Snake	Yang Water	Dog	May	5	15:55
June 6— July 7	Yang Fire	Horse	Yang Water	Dog	June	36	20:40
July 7— August 8	Yin Fire	Sheep	Yang Water	Dog	July	6	7:13
August 8— September 8	Yang Earth	Monkey	Yang Water	Dog	Aug	37	17:05
September 8 – October 9	Yin Earth	Cock	Yang Water	Dog	Sep	8	19:52
October 9— November 9	Yang Metal	Dog	Yang Water	Dog	Oct	38	11:11
November 9- December 7	Yin Metal	Pig	Yang Water	Dog	Nov	9	13:47
December 7 – January 6	Yang Water	Rat	Yang Water	Dog	Dec	39	5:57

1923

	Month		**Year**				
Find your Day Here	Stem	Branch	Stem	Branch	Day	Day	Time
January 6 – February 5	Yin Water	Ox	Yang Water	Dog	Jan	10	16:33
February 5— March 6	Yang Wood	Tiger	Yin Water	Pig	Feb	41	3:58
March 6— April 6	Yin Wood	Rabbit	Yin Water	Pig	Mar	9	22:25
April 6— May 6	Yang Fire	Dragon	Yin Water	Pig	April	40	21:41
May 6 – June 6	Yin Fire	Snake	Yin Water	Pig	May	10	21:28
June 7— July 8	Yang Earth	Horse	Yin Water	Pig	June	41	2:27
July 8— August 8	Yin Earth	Sheep	Yin Water	Pig	July	11	13:01
August 8— September 9	Yang Metal	Monkey	Yin Water	Pig	Aug	42	22:53
September 9 – October 9	Yin Metal	Cock	Yin Water	Pig	Sep	13	1:41
October 9— November 8	Yang Water	Dog	Yin Water	Pig	Oct	43	17:00
November 8— December 8	Yin Water	Pig	Yin Water	Pig	Nov	14	19:30
December 8 – January 6	Yang Wood	Rat	Yin Water	Pig	Dec	44	11:47

Branch	Pig	Rat	Ox	Tiger	Rabbit	Dragon	Snake	Horse	Sheep	Monkey	Cock	Dog
Main Element	Yang Water	Yin Water	Yin Earth	Yang Wood	Yin Wood	Yang Earth	Yang Fire	Yin Fire	Yin Earth	Yang Metal	Yin Metal	Yang Earth
Hidden Elements	Yang Wood		Yin Water Yin Metal	Yang Fire Yang Earth		Yin Wood Yin Water	Yang Earth Yang Metal	Yin Earth	Yin Fire Yin Wood	Yang Earth Yang Water		Yin Metal Yin Fire

1924

	Month		Year				
Find your Day Here	Stem	Branch	Stem	Branch	Day	Day	Time
January 6 – February 5	Yin Wood	Ox	Yin Water	Pig	Jan	15	22:24
February 5-29— March 6	Yang Fire	Tiger	Yang Wood	Rat	Feb	46	9:49
March 6— April 5	Yin Fire	Rabbit	Yang Wood	Rat	Mar	15	4:13
April 5— May 6	Yang Earth	Dragon	Yang Wood	Rat	April	46	9:34
May 6 – June 6	Yin Earth	Snake	Yang Wood	Rat	May	16	3:26
June 6— July 7	Yang Metal	Horse	Yang Wood	Rat	June	47	8:02
July 7— August 8	Yin Metal	Sheep	Yang Wood	Rat	July	17	18:30
August 8— September 8	Yang Water	Monkey	Yang Wood	Rat	Aug	48	4:13
September 8 – October 8	Yin Water	Cock	Yang Wood	Rat	Sep	19	6:46
October 8— November 8	Yang Wood	Dog	Yang Wood	Rat	Oct	49	9:53
November 8—December 7	Yin Wood	Pig	Yang Wood	Rat	Nov	20	:30
December 7 – January 6	Yang Fire	Rat	Yang Wood	Rat	Dec	50	16:54

1925

	Month		Year				
Find your Day Here	Stem	Branch	Stem	Branch	Day	Day	Time
January 6 – February 4	Yin Fire	Ox	Yang Wood	Rat	Jan	21	3:54
February 4— March 6	Yang Earth	Tiger	Yin Wood	Ox	Feb	52	15:37
March 6— April 5	Yin Earth	Rabbit	Yin Wood	Ox	Mar	20	10:00
April 5— May 6	Yang Metal	Dragon	Yin Wood	Ox	April	51	15:23
May 6 – June 6	Yin Metal	Snake	Yin Wood	Ox	May	21	9:18
June 6— July 8	Yang Water	Horse	Yin Wood	Ox	June	52	13:57
July 8— August 8	Yin Water	Sheep	Yin Wood	Ox	July	22	0:25
August 8— September 7	Yang Wood	Monkey	Yin Wood	Ox	Aug	53	10:08
September 8 – October 9	Yin Wood	Cock	Yin Wood	Ox	Sep	24	12:40
October 9— November 8	Yang Fire	Dog	Yin Wood	Ox	Oct	54	3:48
November 8—December 7	Yin Fire	Pig	Yin Wood	Ox	Nov	25	6:27
December 7 – January 6	Yang Earth	Rat	Yin Wood	Ox	Dec	55	22:53

Branch	Pig	Rat	Ox	Tiger	Rabbit	Dragon	Snake	Horse	Sheep	Monkey	Cock	Dog
Main Element	Yang Water	Yin Water	Yin Earth	Yang Wood	Yin Wood	Yang Earth	Yang Fire	Yin Fire	Yin Earth	Yang Metal	Yin Metal	Yang Earth
Hidden Elements	Yang Wood		Yin Water	Yang Fire		Yin Wood	Yang Earth	Yin Earth	Yin Fire	Yang Earth		Yin Metal
			Yin Metal	Yang Earth		Yang Water	Yang Metal		Yin Wood	Yang Water		Yin Fire

1926

Find your Day Here	Month Stem	Branch	Year Stem	Branch	Day	Day	Time
January 6 – February 4	Yin Earth	Ox	Yin Wood	Ox	Jan	26	9:55
February 4— March 5	Yang Metal	Tiger	Yang Fire	Tiger	Feb	57	21:39
March 5— April 5	Yin Metal	Rabbit	Yang Fire	Tiger	Mar	25	15:49
April 5— May 6	Yang Water	Dragon	Yang Fire	Tiger	April	56	21:19
May 6– June 6	Yin Water	Snake	Yang Fire	Tiger	May	26	15:09
June 6— July 8	Yang Wood	Horse	Yang Fire	Tiger	June	57	19:42
July 8— August 8	Yin Wood	Sheep	Yang Fire	Tiger	July	27	6:06
August 8— September 8	Yang Fire	Monkey	Yang Fire	Tiger	Aug	58	15:45
September 8 – October 9	Yin Fire	Cock	Yang Fire	Tiger	Sep	29	18:16
October 9— November 8	Yang Earth	Dog	Yang Fire	Tiger	Oct	59	9:25
November 8—December 8	Yin Earth	Pig	Yang Fire	Tiger	Nov	30	12:08
December 8 – January 6	Yang Metal	Rat	Yang Fire	Tiger	Dec	60	4:39

1927

Find your Day Here	Month Stem	Branch	Year Stem	Branch	Day	Day	Time
January 6 – February 5	Yin Metal	Ox	Yang Fire	Tiger	Jan	31	15:45
February 5— March 7	Yang Water	Tiger	Yin Fire	Rabbit	Feb	2	3:10
March 7— April 6	Yin Water	Rabbit	Yin Fire	Rabbit	Mar	30	21:51
April 6— May 6	Yang Wood	Dragon	Yin Fire	Rabbit	April	1	3:07
May 6 – June 7	Yin Wood	Snake	Yin Fire	Rabbit	May	31	20:54
June 7— July 8	Yang Fire	Horse	Yin Fire	Rabbit	June	2	1:25
July 8— August 8	Yin Fire	Sheep	Yin Fire	Rabbit	July	32	11:50
August 8— September 9	Yang Earth	Monkey	Yin Fire	Rabbit	Aug	3	21:32
September 9 – October 9	Yin Earth	Cock	Yin Fire	Rabbit	Sep	34	0:06
October 9— November 8	Yang Metal	Dog	Yin Fire	Rabbit	Oct	4	15:16
November 8— December 8	Yin Metal	Pig	Yin Fire	Rabbit	Nov	35	17:57
December 8 – January 6	Yang Water	Rat	Yin Fire	Rabbit	Dec	5	10:27

Branch	Pig	Rat	Ox	Tiger	Rabbit	Dragon	Snake	Horse	Sheep	Monkey	Cock	Dog
Main Element	Yang Water	Yin Water	Yin Earth	Yang Wood	Yin Wood	Yang Earth	Yang Fire	Yin Fire	Yin Earth	Yang Metal	Yin Metal	Yang Earth
Hidden Elements	Yang Wood		Yin Water	Yang Fire		Yin Wood	Yang Earth	Yin Earth	Yin Fire	Yang Earth		Yin Metal
			Yin Metal	Yang Earth		Yin Water	Yang Metal		Yin Wood	Yang Water		Yin Fire

1928

	Month		Year				
Find your Day Here	Stem	Branch	Stem	Branch	Day	Day	Time
January 6 – February 5	Yin Water	Ox	Yin Fire	Rabbit	Jan	36	21:32
February 5-29— March 6	Yang Wood	Tiger	Yang Earth	Dragon	Feb	7	9:17
March 6— April 5	Yin Wood	Rabbit	Yang Earth	Dragon	Mar	36	3:38
April 5— May 6	Yang Fire	Dragon	Yang Earth	Dragon	April	7	8:55
May 6 – June 6	Yin Fire	Snake	Yang Earth	Dragon	May	37	2:44
June 6— July 7	Yang Earth	Horse	Yang Earth	Dragon	June	8	7:18
July 7— August 8	Yin Earth	Sheep	Yang Earth	Dragon	July	38	17:45
August 8— September 8	Yang Metal	Monkey	Yang Earth	Dragon	Aug	9	3:28
September 8 – October 8	Yin Metal	Cock	Yang Earth	Dragon	Sep	40	6:02
October 8— November 8	Yang Water	Dog	Yang Earth	Dragon	Oct	10	21:11
November 8— December 7	Yin Water	Pig	Yang Earth	Dragon	Nov	41	23:50
December 7 – January 6	Yang Wood	Rat	Yang Earth	Dragon	Dec	11	16:18

1929

	Month		Year				
Find your Day Here	Stem	Branch	Stem	Branch	Day	Day	Time
January 6 – February 4	Yin Wood	Ox	Yang Earth	Dragon	Jan	42	3:23
February 4— March 6	Yang Fire	Tiger	Yin Earth	Snake	Feb	13	15:09
March 6— April 5	Yin Fire	Rabbit	Yin Earth	Snake	Mar	41	9:32
April 5— May 6	Yang Earth	Dragon	Yin Earth	Snake	April	12	14:52
May 6 – June 6	Yin Earth	Snake	Yin Earth	Snake	May	42	8:41
June 6— July 8	Yang Metal	Horse	Yin Earth	Snake	June	13	13:11
July 8— August 8	Yin Metal	Sheep	Yin Earth	Snake	July	43	23:32
August 8— September 8	Yang Water	Monkey	Yin Earth	Snake	Aug	14	9:09
September 8 – October 9	Yin Water	Cock	Yin Earth	Snake	Sep	45	11:40
October 9— November 8	Yang Wood	Dog	Yin Earth	Snake	Oct	15	2:48
November 8— December 7	Yin Wood	Pig	Yin Earth	Snake	Nov	46	5:28
December 7 – January 6	Yang Fire	Rat	Yin Earth	Snake	Dec	16	21:57

Branch	Pig	Rat	Ox	Tiger	Rabbit	Dragon	Snake	Horse	Sheep	Monkey	Cock	Dog
Main Element	Yang Water	Yin Water	Yin Earth	Yang Wood	Yin Wood	Yang Earth	Yang Fire	Yin Fire	Yin Earth	Yang Metal	Yin Metal	Yang Earth
Hidden Elements	Yang Wood		Yin Water	Yang Fire		Yin Wood	Yang Earth	Yin Earth	Yin Fire	Yang Earth		Yin Metal
			Yin Metal	Yang Earth		Yin Water	Yang Metal		Yin Wood	Yang Water		Yin Fire

1930

	Month		**Year**				
Find Your Day Here	Stem	Branch	Stem	Branch	Day	Day	Time
January 6 – February 4	Yin Fire	Ox	Yin Earth	Snake	Jan	47	9: 03
February 4— March 6	Yang Earth	Tiger	Yang Metal	Horse	Feb	18	20: 52
March 6— April 5	Yin Earth	Rabbit	Yang Metal	Horse	Mar	46	15: 17
April 5— May 6	Yang Metal	Dragon	Yang Metal	Horse	April	17	20: 38
May 6– June 6	Yin Metal	Snake	Yang Metal	Horse	May	47	14: 28
June 6— July 8	Yang Water	Horse	Yang Metal	Horse	June	18	18: 58
July 8— August 8	Yin Water	Sheep	Yang Metal	Horse	July	48	5: 20
August 8— September 8	Yang Wood	Monkey	Yang Metal	Horse	Aug	19	14: 58
September 8 – October 9	Yin Wood	Cock	Yang Metal	Horse	Sep	50	17:29
October 9— November 8	Yang Fire	Dog	Yang Metal	Horse	Oct	20	8:38
November 8— December 8	Yin Fire	Pig	Yang Metal	Horse	Nov	51	11: 21
December 8 – January 6	Yang Earth	Rat	Yang Metal	Horse	Dec	21	3:51

1931

	Month		**Year**				
Find Your Day Here	Stem	Branch	Stem	Branch	Day	Day	Time
January 6 – February 5	Yin Earth	Ox	Yang Metal	Horse	Jan	52	14:56
February 5— March 7	Yang Metal	Tiger	Yin Metal	Sheep	Feb	23	2: 41
March 7— April 6	Yin Metal	Rabbit	Yin Metal	Sheep	Mar	51	21: 03
April 6— May 7	Yang Water	Dragon	Yin Metal	Sheep	April	22	2: 21
May 7 – June 7	Yin Water	Snake	Yin Metal	Sheep	May	52	20: 10
June 7— July 8	Yang Wood	Horse	Yin Metal	Sheep	June	23	: 42
July 8— August 8	Yin Wood	Sheep	Yin Metal	Sheep	July	53	11: 06
August 8— September 9	Yang Fire	Monkey	Yin Metal	Sheep	Aug	24	20: 45
September 9 – October 9	Yin Fire	Cock	Yin Metal	Sheep	Sep	55	23:18
October 9— November 8	Yang Earth	Dog	Yin Metal	Sheep	Oct	25	14:27
November 8— December 8	Yin Earth	Pig	Yin Metal	Sheep	Nov	56	17: 10
December 8 – January 6	Yang Metal	Rat	Yin Metal	Sheep	Dec	26	9: 41

Branch	Pig	Rat	Ox	Tiger	Rabbit	Dragon	Snake	Horse	Sheep	Monkey	Cock	Dog
Main Element	Yang Water	Yin Water	Yin Earth	Yang Wood	Yin Wood	Yang Earth	Yang Fire	Yin Fire	Yin Earth	Yang Metal	Yin Metal	Yang Earth
Hidden Elements	Yang Wood		Yin Water	Yang Fire		Yin Wood	Yang Earth	Yin Earth	Yin Fire	Yang Earth		Yin Metal
			Yin Metal	Yang Earth		Yin Water	Yang Metal		Yin Wood	Yang Water		Yin Fire

1932

Find Your Day Here	Month Stem	Branch	Year Stem	Branch	Day	Day	Time
January 6– February 5	Yin Metal	Ox	Yin Metal	Sheep	Jan	57	20:46
February 5-29, — March 6	Yang Water	Tiger	Yang Water	Monkey	Feb	28	8:30
March 6— April 5	Yin Water	Rabbit	Yang Water	Monkey	Mar	57	2:50
April 5— May 6	Yang Wood	Dragon	Yang Water	Monkey	April	28	8:07
May 6 – June 6	Yin Wood	Snake	Yang Water	Monkey	May	58	1:55
June 6— July 7	Yang Fire	Horse	Yang Water	Monkey	June	29	6:28
July 7— August 8	Yin Fire	Sheep	Yang Water	Monkey	July	59	16:53
August 8— September 8	Yang Earth	Monkey	Yang Water	Monkey	Aug	30	2:32
September 8 – October 8	Yin Earth	Cock	Yang Water	Monkey	Sep	1	5:03
October 8— November 7	Yang Metal	Dog	Yang Water	Monkey	Oct	31	20:10
November 7— December 7	Yin Metal	Pig	Yang Water	Monkey	Nov	2	22:50
December 7 – January 6	Yang Water	Rat	Yang Water	Monkey	Dec	32	15:19

1933

Find Your Day Here	Month Stem	Branch	Year Stem	Branch	Day	Day	Time
January 6 – February 4	Yin Water	Ox	Yang Water	Monkey	Jan	57	2: 24
February 4 —March 6	Yang Wood	Tiger	Yin Water	Cock	Feb	28	14: 10
March 6 – April 5	Yin Wood	Rabbit	Yin Water	Cock	Mar	57	8: 32
April 5 – May 6	Yang Fire	Dragon	Yin Water	Cock	April	28	13: 51
May 6 – June 6	Yin Fire	Snake	Yin Water	Cock	May	58	7: 42
June 6 – July 7	Yang Earth	Horse	Yin Water	Cock	June	29	12: 18
July 7 – August 8	Yin Earth	Sheep	Yin Water	Cock	July	59	22: 45
August 8– September 8	Yang Metal	Monkey	Yin Water	Cock	Aug	30	8:26
September 8 – October 9	Yin Metal	Cock	Yin Water	Cock	Sep	1	10:58
October 9 – November 8	Yang Water	Dog	Yin Water	Cock	Oct	31	2:08
November 8 – December 7	Yin Water	Pig	Yin Water	Cock	Nov	2	4:44
December 7 – January 6	Yang Wood	Rat	Yin Water	Cock	Dec	32	21:12

Branch	Pig	Rat	Ox	Tiger	Rabbit	Dragon	Snake	Horse	Sheep	Monkey	Cock	Dog
Main Element	Yang Water	Yin Water	Yin Earth	Yang Wood	Yin Wood	Yang Earth	Yang Fire	Yin Fire	Yin Earth	Yang Metal	Yin Metal	Yang Earth
Hidden Elements	Yang Wood		Yin Water	Yang Fire		Yin Wood	Yang Earth	Yin Earth	Yin Fire	Yang Earth		Yin Metal
			Yin Metal	Yang Earth		Yin Water	Yang Metal		Yin Wood	Yang Water		Yin Fire

1934

	Month		**Year**				
Find Your Day Here Stem		Branch	Stem	Branch	Day	Day	Time
January 6– February 4	Yin Wood	Ox	Yin Water	Cock	Jan	8	8: 17
February 4— March 6	Yang Fire	Tiger	Yang Wood	Dog	Feb	39	20: 04
March 6— April 5	Yin Fire	Rabbit	Yang Wood	Dog	Mar	7	14: 27
April 5— May 6	Yang Earth	Dragon	Yang Wood	Dog	April	38	19: 44
May 6 – June 6	Yin Earth	Snake	Yang Wood	Dog	May	8	13: 31
June 6— July 8	Yang Metal	Horse	Yang Wood	Dog	June	39	18: 02
July 8— August 8	Yin Metal	Sheep	Yang Wood	Dog	July	9	4: 25
August 8— September 8	Yang Water	Monkey	Yang Wood	Dog	Aug	40	14:04
September 8 – October 9	Yin Water	Cock	Yang Wood	Dog	Sep	11	16: 37
October 9— November 8	Yang Wood	Dog	Yang Wood	Dog	Oct	41	7: 45
November 8— December 8	Yin Wood	Pig	Yang Wood	Dog	Nov	12	10: 27
December 8 – January 6	Yang Fire	Rat	Yang Wood	Dog	Dec	42	2:57

1935

	Month		**Year**				
Find your Day Here Stem		Branch	Stem	Branch	Day	Day	Time
January 6– February 5	Yin Fire	Ox	Yang Wood	Dog	Jan	13	14: 03
February 5— March 6	Yang Earth	Tiger	Yin Wood	Pig	Feb	44	1: 49
March 6— April 6	Yin Earth	Rabbit	Yin Wood	Pig	Mar	12	20: 11
April 6— May 6	Yang Metal	Dragon	Yin Wood	Pig	April	43	1: 27
May 6– June 7	Yin Metal	Snake	Yin Wood	Pig	May	13	19:12
June 7— July 8	Yang Water	Horse	Yin Wood	Pig	June	44	23:42
July 8— August 8	Yin Water	Sheep	Yin Wood	Pig	July	14	10: 06
August 8— September 8	Yang Wood	Monkey	Yin Wood	Pig	Aug	45	19: 48
September 8 – October 9	Yin Wood	Cock	Yin Wood	Pig	Sep	16	23: 25
October 9— November 8	Yang Fire	Dog	Yin Wood	Pig	Oct	46	13: 36
November 8— December 8	Yin Fire	Pig	Yin Wood	Pig	Nov	17	16: 18
December 8 – January 6	Yang Earth	Rat	Yin Wood	Pig	Dec	47	8: 45

Branch	Pig	Rat	Ox	Tiger	Rabbit	Dragon	Snake	Horse	Sheep	Monkey	Cock	Dog
Main Element	Yang Water	Yin Water	Yin Earth	Yang Wood	Yin Wood	Yang Earth	Yang Fire	Yin Fire	Yin Earth	Yang Metal	Yin Metal	Yang Earth
Hidden Elements	Yang Wood		Yin Water	Yang Fire		Yin Wood	Yang Earth	Yin Earth	Yin Fire	Yang Earth		Yin Metal
			Yin Metal	Yang Earth		Yin Water	Yang Metal		Yin Wood	Yang Water		Yin Fire

1936

	Month		Year				
Find your Day Here	**Stem**	**Branch**	**Stem**	**Branch**	**Day**	**Day**	**Time**
January 6 – February 5	Yin Earth	Ox	Yin Wood	Pig	Jan	18	19: 47
February 5 – 29,— March 6	Yang Metal	Tiger	Yang Fire	Rat	Feb	49	7: 29
March 6— April 5	Yin Metal	Rabbit	Yang Fire	Rat	Mar	18	1: 50
April 5— May 6	Yang Water	Dragon	Yang Fire	Rat	April	49	7: 07
May 6 – June 6	Yin Water	Snake	Yang Fire	Rat	May	19	: 57
June 6— July 7	Yang Wood	Horse	Yang Fire	Rat	June	50	5: 31
July 7— August 8	Yin Wood	Sheep	Yang Fire	Rat	July	20	15: 59
August 8— September 8	Yang Fire	Monkey	Yang Fire	Rat	Aug	51	1: 43
September 8 – October 8	Yin Fire	Cock	Yang Fire	Rat	Sep	22	4:21
October 8— November 7	Yang Earth	Dog	Yang Fire	Rat	Oct	52	19: 33
November 7— December 7	Yin Earth	Pig	Yang Fire	Rat	Nov	23	22:15
December 7 – January 6	Yang Metal	Rat	Yang Fire	Rat	Dec	53	14:43

1937

	Month		Year				
Find your Day Here	**Stem**	**Branch**	**Stem**	**Branch**	**Day**	**Day**	**Time**
January 6— February 4	Yin Metal	Ox	Yang Fire	Rat	Jan	24	1: 44
February 4 —March 6	Yang Water	Tiger	Yin Fire	Ox	Feb	55	13: 26
March 6 – April 5	Yin Water	Rabbit	Yin Fire	Ox	Mar	23	7: 45
April 5 – May 6	Yang Wood	Dragon	Yin Fire	Ox	April	54	13: 02
May 6 – June 6	Yin Wood	Snake	Yin Fire	Ox	May	24	6: 51
June 6 – July 7	Yang Fire	Horse	Yin Fire	Ox	June	55	11: 23
July 7– August 8	Yin Fire	Sheep	Yin Fire	Ox	July	25	21: 46
August 8– September 8	Yang Earth	Monkey	Yin Fire	Ox	Aug	56	7: 26
September 8 – October 9	Yin Earth	Cock	Yin Fire	Ox	Sep	27	10: 00
October 9 – November 8	Yang Metal	Dog	Yin Fire	Ox	Oct	57	1: 11
November 8 – December 7	Yin Metal	Pig	Yin Fire	Ox	Nov	28	3: 46
December 7 – January 6	Yang Water	Rat	Yin Fire	Ox	Dec	58	20: 27

Branch	Pig	Rat	Ox	Tiger	Rabbit	Dragon	Snake	Horse	Sheep	Monkey	Cock	Dog
Main Element	Yang Water	Yin Water	Yin Earth	Yang Wood	Yin Wood	Yang Earth	Yang Fire	Yin Fire	Yin Earth	Yang Metal	Yin Metal	Yang Earth
Hidden Elements	Yang Wood		Yin Water	Yang Fire		Yin Wood	Yang Earth	Yin Earth	Yin Fire	Yang Earth		Yin Metal
				Yang Earth								
			Yin Metal			Yin Water	Yang Metal		Yin Wood	Yang Water		Yin Fire

1938

Find your Day Here	Month Stem	Branch	Year Stem	Branch	Day	Day	Time
January 6 – February 4	Yin Water	Ox	Yin Fire	Ox	Jan	29	7: 32
February 4— March 6	Yang Wood	Tiger	Yang Earth	Tiger	Feb	60	19:15
March 6— April 5	Yin Wood	Rabbit	Yang Earth	Tiger	Mar	28	13: 34
April 5— May 6	Yang Fire	Dragon	Yang Earth	Tiger	April	59	18: 49
May 6– June 6	Yin Fire	Snake	Yang Earth	Tiger	May	29	12: 36
June 6— July 8	Yang Earth	Horse	Yang Earth	Tiger	June	60	17: 07
July 8— August 8	Yin Earth	Sheep	Yang Earth	Tiger	July	30	3: 32
August 8— September 8	Yang Metal	Monkey	Yang Earth	Tiger	Aug	1	13: 13
September 8 – October 9	Yin Metal	Cock	Yang Earth	Tiger	Sep	32	15: 49
October 9— November 8	Yang Water	Dog	Yang Earth	Tiger	Oct	2	7: 02
November 8— December 8	Yin Water	Pig	Yang Earth	Tiger	Nov	33	9: 49
December 8 – January 6	Yang Wood	Rat	Yang Earth	Tiger	Dec	3	2: 23

1939

Find your Day Here	Month Stem	Branch	Year Stem	Branch	Day	Day	Time
January 6 – February 5	Yin Wood	Ox	Yang Earth	Tiger	Jan	34	13: 23
February 5— March 6	Yang Fire	Tiger	Yin Earth	Rabbit	Feb	5	1: 11
March 6 —April 6	Yin Fire	Rabbit	Yin Earth	Rabbit	Mar	33	19: 27
April 6— May 6	Yang Earth	Dragon	Yin Earth	Rabbit	April	4	: 38
May 6 – June 6	Yin Earth	Snake	Yin Earth	Rabbit	May	34	18: 21
June 6— July 8	Yang Metal	Horse	Yin Earth	Rabbit	June	5	22: 52
July 8— August 8	Yin Metal	Sheep	Yin Earth	Rabbit	July	35	9: 19
August 8— September 8	Yang Water	Monkey	Yin Earth	Rabbit	Aug	6	19: 04
September 8 – October 9	Yin Water	Cock	Yin Earth	Rabbit	Sep	37	21: 42
October 9— November 8	Yang Wood	Dog	Yin Earth	Rabbit	Oct	7	12: 57
November 8— December 8	Yin Wood	Pig	Yin Earth	Rabbit	Nov	38	15: 40
December 8 – January 6	Yang Fire	Rat	Yin Earth	Rabbit	Dec	8	8:18

Branch	Pig	Rat	Ox	Tiger	Rabbit	Dragon	Snake	Horse	Sheep	Monkey	Cock	Dog
Main Element	Yang Water	Yin Water	Yin Earth	Yang Wood	Yin Wood	Yang Earth	Yang Fire	Yin Fire	Yin Earth	Yang Metal	Yin Metal	Yang Earth
Hidden Elements	Yang Wood		Yin Water Yin Metal	Yang Fire Yang Earth		Yin Wood Yin Water	Yang Earth Yang Metal	Yin Earth	Yin Fire Yin Wood	Yang Earth Yang Water		Yin Metal Yin Fire

1940

	Month		Year				
Find your Day Here	Stem	Branch	Stem	Branch	Day	Day	Time
January 6 – February 5	Yin Fire	Ox	Yin Earth	Rabbit	Jan	39	19:24
February 5—29, March 6	Yang Earth	Tiger	Yang Metal	Dragon	Feb	10	7:08
March 6—April 5	Yin Earth	Rabbit	Yang Metal	Dragon	Mar	39	1:24
April 5 – May 6	Yang Metal	Dragon	Yang Metal	Dragon	April	10	6:35
May 6 – June 6	Yin Metal	Snake	Yang Metal	Dragon	May	40	:16
June 6 – July 7	Yang Water	Horse	Yang Metal	Dragon	June	11	4:44
July 7 – August 8	Yin Water	Sheep	Yang Metal	Dragon	July	41	15:08
August 8 – September 8	Yang Wood	Monkey	Yang Metal	Dragon	Aug	12	:52
September 8 – October 8	Yin Wood	Cock	Yang Metal	Dragon	Sep	43	3:30
October 8 – November 7	Yang Fire	Dog	Yang Metal	Dragon	Oct	13	18:43
November 7 – December 7	Yin Fire	Pig	Yang Metal	Dragon	Nov	44	21:27
December 7 – January 6	Yang Earth	Rat	Yang Metal	Dragon	Dec	14	13:58

1941

	Month		Year				
Find your Day Here	Stem	Branch	Stem	Branch	Day	Day	Time
January 6 – February 4	Yin Earth	Ox	Yang Metal	Dragon	Jan	45	1:04
February 4 – March 6	Yang Metal	Tiger	Yin Metal	Snake	Feb	16	12:50
March 6 – April 5	Yin Metal	Rabbit	Yin Metal	Snake	Mar	44	7:10
April 5 – May 6	Yang Water	Dragon	Yin Metal	Snake	April	15	12:25
May 6 – June 6	Yin Water	Snake	Yin Metal	Snake	May	45	6:10
June 6 – July 7	Yang Wood	Horse	Yin Metal	Snake	June	16	10:40
July 7 – August 8	Yin Wood	Sheep	Yin Metal	Snake	July	46	21:03
August 8 – September 8	Yang Fire	Monkey	Yin Metal	Snake	Aug	17	6:46
September 8 – October 9	Yin Fire	Cock	Yin Metal	Snake	Sep	48	9:24
October 9 – November 8	Yang Earth	Dog	Yin Metal	Snake	Oct	18	:39
November 8 – December 7	Yin Earth	Pig	Yin Metal	Snake	Nov	49	3:25
December 7 – January 6	Yang Metal	Rat	Yin Metal	Snake	Dec	19	19:57

Branch	Pig	Rat	Ox	Tiger	Rabbit	Dragon	Snake	Horse	Sheep	Monkey	Cock	Dog
Main Element	Yang Water	Yin Water	Yin Earth	Yang Wood	Yin Wood	Yang Earth	Yang Fire	Yin Fire	Yin Earth	Yang Metal	Yin Metal	Yang Earth
Hidden Elements	Yang Wood		Yin Water	Yang Fire		Yin Wood	Yang Earth	Yin Earth	Yin Fire	Yang Earth		Yin Metal
			Yin Metal	Yang Earth		Yin Water	Yang Metal		Yin Wood	Yang Water		Yin Fire

1942

Find your Day Here	Month Stem	Branch	Year Stem	Branch	Day	Day	Time
January 6 – February 4	Yin Metal	Ox	Yin Metal	Snake	Jan	50	7:03
February 4 – March 6	Yang Water	Tiger	Yang Water	Horse	Feb	21	18:49
March 6 – April 5	Yin Water	Rabbit	Yang Water	Horse	Mar	49	13:10
April 5 – May 6	Yang Wood	Dragon	Yang Water	Horse	April	20	18:24
May 6 – June 6	Yin Wood	Snake	Yang Water	Horse	May	50	12:07
June 6 – July 8	Yang Fire	Horse	Yang Water	Horse	June	21	16:37
July 8 – August 8	Yin Fire	Sheep	Yang Water	Horse	July	51	2:52
August 8 – September 8	Yang Earth	Monkey	Yang Water	Horse	Aug	22	12:31
September 8 – October 9	Yin Earth	Cock	Yang Water	Horse	Sep	53	15:07
October 9 – November 8	Yang Metal	Dog	Yang Water	Horse	Oct	23	6:22
November 8 – December 8	Yin Metal	Pig	Yang Water	Horse	Nov	54	9:12
December 8 – January 6	Yang Water	Rat	Yang Water	Horse	Dec	24	1:47

1943

Find your Day Here	Month Stem	Branch	Year Stem	Branch	Day	Day	Time
January 6 –February 5	Yin Water	Ox	Yang Water	Horse	Jan	55	12:55
February 5 – March 6	Yang Wood	Tiger	Yin Water	Sheep	Feb	26	: 40
March 6 – April 6	Yin Wood	Rabbit	Yin Water	Sheep	Mar	54	18: 59
April 6 – May 6	Yang Fire	Dragon	Yin Water	Sheep	April	25	: 12
May 6 – June 6	Yin Fire	Snake	Yin Water	Sheep	May	55	17:54
June 6 – July 8	Yang Earth	Horse	Yin Water	Sheep	June	26	22 19
July 8 – August 8	Yin Earth	Sheep	Yin Water	Sheep	July	56	8:39
August 8 – September 8	Yang Metal	Monkey	Yin Water	Sheep	Aug	27	18: 19
September 8 – October 9	Yin Metal	Cock	Yin Water	Sheep	Sep	58	20: 56
October 9 – November 8	Yang Water	Dog	Yin Water	Sheep	Oct	28	12: 11
November 8 – December 8	Yin Water	Pig	Yin Water	Sheep	Nov	59	14: 59
December 8 – January 6	Yang Wood	Rat	Yin Water	Sheep	Dec	29	7: 33

Branch	Pig	Rat	Ox	Tiger	Rabbit	Dragon	Snake	Horse	Sheep	Monkey	Cock	Dog
Main Element	Yang Water	Yin Water	Yin Earth	Yang Wood	Yin Wood	Yang Earth	Yang Fire	Yin Fire	Yin Earth	Yang Metal	Yin Metal	Yang Earth
Hidden Elements	Yang Wood		Yin Water	Yang Fire		Yin Wood	Yang Earth	Yin Earth	Yin Fire	Yang Earth		Yin Metal
			Yin Metal	Yang Earth		Yin Water	Yang Metal		Yin Wood	Yang Water		Yin Fire

1944

Find your Day Here	Month		Year		Day	Day	Time
	Stem	Branch	Stem	Branch			
January 6 – February 5	Yin Wood	Ox	Yin Water	Sheep	Jan	60	18: 44
February 5-29, March 6	Yang Fire	Tiger	Yang Wood	Monkey	Feb	31	6: 23
March 6—April 5	Yin Fire	Rabbit	Yang Wood	Monkey	Mar	60	: 41
April 5—May 6	Yang Earth	Dragon	Yang Wood	Monkey	April	31	5: 54
May 6—June 6	Yin Earth	Snake	Yang Wood	Monkey	May	1	23: 40
June 6—July 7	Yang Metal	Horse	Yang Wood	Monkey	June	32	4: 11
July 7—August 8	Yin Metal	Sheep	Yang Wood	Monkey	July	2	14: 37
August 8— September 8	Yang Water	Monkey	Yang Wood	Monkey	Aug	33	: 19
September 8—October 8	Yin Water	Cock	Yang Wood	Monkey	Sep	4	2:56
October 8— November 7	Yang Wood	Dog	Yang Wood	Monkey	Oct	34	18:09
November 7— December 7	Yin Wood	Pig	Yang Wood	Monkey	Nov	5	20: 55
December 7—January 6	Yang Fire	Rat	Yang Wood	Monkey	Dec	35	13: 28

1945

Find your Day Here	Month		Year		Day	Day	Time
	Stem	Branch	Stem	Branch			
January 6 – February 4	Yin Fire	Ox	Yang Wood	Monkey	Jan	6	:35
February 4— March 6	Yang Earth	Tiger	Yin Wood	Cock	Feb	37	12:20
March 6—April 5	Yin Earth	Rabbit	Yin Wood	Cock	Mar	5	6:38
April 5— May 6	Yang Metal	Dragon	Yin Wood	Cock	April	36	11:52
May 6 – June 6	Yin Metal	Snake	Yin Wood	Cock	May	6	5:37
June 6 – July 7	Yang Water	Horse	Yin Wood	Cock	June	37	10:06
July 7— August 8	Yin Water	Sheep	Yin Wood	Cock	July	7	20:27
August 8—September 8	Yang Wood	Monkey	Yin Wood	Cock	Aug	38	6:06
September 8— October 9	Yin Wood	Cock	Yin Wood	Cock	Sep	9	8:39
October 9— November 8	Yang Fire	Dog	Yin Wood	Cock	Oct	39	23:50
November 8—December 7	Yin Fire	Pig	Yin Wood	Cock	Nov	10	2:35
December 7— January 6	Yang Earth	Rat	Yin Wood	Cock	Dec	40	19:08

Branch	Pig	Rat	Ox	Tiger	Rabbit	Dragon	Snake	Horse	Sheep	Monkey	Cock	Dog
Main Element	Yang Water	Yin Water	Yin Earth	Yang Wood	Yin Wood	Yang Earth	Yang Fire	Yin Fire	Yin Earth	Yang Metal	Yin Metal	Yang Earth
Hidden Elements	Yang Wood		Yin Water	Yang Fire		Yin Wood	Yang Earth	Yin Earth	Yin Fire	Yang Earth		Yin Metal
			Yin Metal	Yang Earth			Yin Water	Yang Metal		Yin Wood		Yin Fire
									Yang Water	

1946

Find your Day Here	Month Stem	Branch	Year Stem	Branch	Day	Day	Time
January 6 – February 4	Yin Earth	Ox	Yin Wood	Cock	Jan	11	6:17
February 4— March 6	Yang Metal	Tiger	Yang Fire	Dog	Feb	42	18:04
March 6—April 5	Yin Metal	Rabbit	Yang Fire	Dog	Mar	10	12:25
April 5— May 6	Yang Water	Dragon	Yang Fire	Dog	April	41	17:39
May 6 – June 6	Yin Water	Snake	Yang Fire	Dog	May	11	11:22
June 6 – July 8	Yang Wood	Horse	Yang Fire	Dog	June	42	15:49
July 8— August 8	Yin Wood	Sheep	Yang Fire	Dog	July	12	2:11
August 8—September 8	Yang Fire	Monkey	Yang Fire	Dog	Aug	43	11:52
September 8— October 9	Yin Fire	Cock	Yang Fire	Dog	Sep	14	14:28
October 9— November 8	Yang Earth	Dog	Yang Fire	Dog	Oct	44	5:42
November 8—December 8	Yin Earth	Pig	Yang Fire	Dog	Nov	15	8:28
December 8— January 6	Yang Metal	Rat	Yang Fire	Dog	Dec	45	1:01

1947

Find your Day Here	Month Stem	Branch	Year Stem	Branch	Day	Day	Time
January 6 – February 5	Yin Metal	Ox	Yang Fire	Dog	Jan	16	12:11
February 5- March 6	Yang Water	Tiger	Yin Fire	Pig	Feb	47	23:55
March 6—April 6	Yin Water	Rabbit	Yin Fire	Pig	Mar	15	18:12
April 6—May 6	Yang Wood	Dragon	Yin Fire	Pig	April	46	23:23
May 6—June 6	Yin Wood	Snake	Yin Fire	Pig	May	16	17:05
June 6—July 8	Yang Fire	Horse	Yin Fire	Pig	June	47	21:33
July 8—August 8	Yin Fire	Sheep	Yin Fire	Pig	July	17	7:56
August 8—September 8	Yang Earth	Monkey	Yin Fire	Pig	Aug	48	17:39
September 8—October 9	Yin Earth	Cock	Yin Fire	Pig	Sep	19	21:07
October 9—November 8	Yang Metal	Dog	Yin Fire	Pig	Oct	49	11:32
November 8- December 8	Yin Metal	Pig	Yin Fire	Pig	Nov	20	14:19
December 8—January 6	Yang Water	Rat	Yin Fire	Pig	Dec	50	6:53

Branch	Pig	Rat	Ox	Tiger	Rabbit	Dragon	Snake	Horse	Sheep	Monkey	Cock	Dog
Main Element	Yang Water	Yin Water	Yin Earth	Yang Wood	Yin Wood	Yang Earth	Yang Fire	Yin Fire	Yin Earth	Yang Metal	Yin Metal	Yang Earth
Hidden Elements	Yang Wood		Yin Water	Yang Fire		Yin Wood	Yang Earth	Yin Earth	Yin Fire	Yang Earth		Yin Metal
			Yin Metal	Yang Earth		Yin Water	Yang Metal		Yin Wood	Yang Water		Yin Fire

1948

	Month		Year				
Find your Day Here	Stem	Branch	Stem	Branch	Day	Day	Time
January 6 – February 5	Yin Water	Ox	Yin Fire	Pig	Jan	21	18:01
February 5—29, March 6	Yang Wood	Tiger	Yang Earth	Rat	Feb	52	5:42
March 6—April 5	Yin Wood	Rabbit	Yang Earth	Rat	Mar	21	23:58
April 5—May 5	Yang Fire	Dragon	Yang Earth	Rat	April	52	5:10
May 5—June 6	Yin Fire	Snake	Yang Earth	Rat	May	22	22:53
June 6—July 7	Yang Earth	Horse	Yang Earth	Rat	June	53	3:21
July 7—August 8	Yin Earth	Sheep	Yang Earth	Rat	July	23	13:44
August 8—September 8	Yang Metal	Monkey	Yang Earth	Rat	Aug	54	23:27
September 8—October 8	Yin Metal	Cock	Yang Earth	Rat	Sep	25	2:06
October 8—November 7	Yang Water	Dog	Yang Earth	Rat	Oct	55	17:21
November 7—December 7	Yin Water	Pig	Yang Earth	Rat	Nov	26	20:07
December 7—January 6	Yang Wood	Rat	Yang Earth	Rat	Dec	56	12:38

1949

	Month		Year				
Find your Day Here	Stem	Branch	Stem	Branch	Day	Day	Time
January 6 – February 4	Yin Wood	Ox	Yang Earth	Rat	Jan	27	23:42
February 4—March 6	Yang Fire	Tiger	Yin Earth	Ox	Feb	58	11:23
March 6—April 5	Yin Fire	Rabbit	Yin Earth	Ox	Mar	26	5:40
April 5—May 6	Yang Earth	Dragon	Yin Earth	Ox	April	57	10:52
May 6—June 6	Yin Earth	Snake	Yin Earth	Ox	May	27	4:37
June 6—July 7	Yang Metal	Horse	Yin Earth	Ox	June	58	9:07
July 7—August 8	Yin Metal	Sheep	Yin Earth	Ox	July	28	19:32
August 8—September 8	Yang Water	Monkey	Yin Earth	Ox	Aug	59	5:16
September 8—October 8	Yin Water	Cock	Yin Earth	Ox	Sep	30	7:55
October 8 – November 8	Yang Wood	Dog	Yin Earth	Ox	Oct	60	23:12
November 8 – December 7	Yin Wood	Pig	Yin Earth	Ox	Nov	31	2:00
December 7 – January 6	Yang Fire	Rat	Yin Earth	Ox	Dec	1	18:34

Branch	Pig	Rat	Ox	Tiger	Rabbit	Dragon	Snake	Horse	Sheep	Monkey	Cock	Dog
Main Element	Yang Water	Yin Water	Yin Earth	Yang Wood	Yin Wood	Yang Earth	Yang Fire	Yang Fire	Yin Earth	Yang Metal	Yin Metal	Yang Earth
Hidden Elements	Yang Wood		Yin Water	Yang Fire		Yin Wood	Yang Earth	Yin Earth	Yin Fire	Yang Earth		Yin Metal
			Yin Metal	Yang Earth		Yin Water	Yang Metal		Yin Wood	Yang Water		Yin Fire

1950

	Month		Year				
Find your Day Here	Stem	Branch	Stem	Branch	Day	Day	Time
January 6- February 4	Yin Fire	Ox	Yin Earth	Ox	Jan	32	5: 39
February 4 – March 6	Yang Earth	Tiger	Yang Metal	Tiger	Feb	3	17: 21
March 6 – April 5	Yin Earth	Rabbit	Yang Metal	Tiger	Mar	31	11: 36
April 5 – May 6	Yang Metal	Dragon	Yang Metal	Tiger	April	2	16: 45
May 6 – June 6	Yin Metal	Snake	Yang Metal	Tiger	May	32	10: 25
June 6 – July 8	Yang Water	Horse	Yang Metal	Tiger	June	3	14: 52
July 8 – August 8	Yin Water	Sheep	Yang Metal	Tiger	July	33	1: 14
August 8 – September 8	Yang Wood	Monkey	Yang Metal	Tiger	Aug	4	10:56
September 8 – October 9	Yin Wood	Cock	Yang Metal	Tiger	Sep	35	13: 34
October 9 – November 8	Yang Fire	Dog	Yang Metal	Tiger	Oct	5	4:52
November 8 – December 8	Yin Fire	Pig	Yang Metal	Tiger	Nov	36	7: 44
December 8 – January 6	Yang Earth	Rat	Yang Metal	Tiger	Dec	6	: 22

1951

	Month		Year				
Find your Day Here	Stem	Branch	Stem	Branch	Day	Day	Time
January 6- February 4	Yin Earth	Ox	Yang Metal	Tiger	Jan	37	11:31
February 4 – March 6	Yang Metal	Tiger	Yin Metal	Rabbit	Feb	8	23:14
March 6 – April 5	Yin Metal	Rabbit	Yin Metal	Rabbit	Mar	36	17:27
April 5 – May 6	Yang Water	Dragon	Yin Metal	Rabbit	April	7	22:33
May 6 – June 6	Yin Water	Snake	Yin Metal	Rabbit	May	37	16:10
June 6 – July 8	Yang Wood	Horse	Yin Metal	Rabbit	June	8	20:33
July 8 – August 8	Yin Wood	Sheep	Yin Metal	Rabbit	July	38	6:54
August 8 – September 8	Yang Fire	Monkey	Yin Metal	Rabbit	Aug	9	16:38
September 8 – October 9	Yin Fire	Cock	Yin Metal	Rabbit	Sep	40	19:19
October 9 – November 8	Yang Earth	Dog	Yin Metal	Rabbit	Oct	10	10:37
November 8 – December 8	Yin Earth	Pig	Yin Metal	Rabbit	Nov	41	13:27
December 8 – January 6	Yang Metal	Rat	Yin Metal	Rabbit	Dec	11	6:03

Branch	Pig	Rat	Ox	Tiger	Rabbit	Dragon	Snake	Horse	Sheep	Monkey	Cock	Dog
Main Element	Yang Water	Yin Water	Yin Earth	Yang Wood	Yin Wood	Yang Earth	Yang Fire	Yin Fire	Yin Earth	Yang Metal	Yin Metal	Yang Earth
Hidden Elements	Yang Wood		Yin Water	Yang Fire		Yin Wood	Yang Earth	Yin Earth	Yin Fire	Yang Earth		Yin Metal
			Yin Metal	Yang Earth		Yin Water	Yang Metal		Yin Wood	Yang Water		Yin Fire

1952

	Month		Year				
Find your Day Here	Stem	Branch	Stem	Branch	Day	Day	Time
January 6- February 5	Yin Metal	Ox	Yin Metal	Rabbit	Jan	42	17:10
February 5 – 29, March 6	Yang Water	Tiger	Yang Water	Dragon	Feb	13	4:53
March 6 – April 5	Yin Water	Rabbit	Yang Water	Dragon	Mar	42	23:08
April 5 – May 5	Yang Wood	Dragon	Yang Water	Dragon	April	13	4:16
May 5 – June 6	Yin Wood	Snake	Yang Water	Dragon	May	43	21:54
June 6 – July 7	Yang Fire	Horse	Yang Water	Dragon	June	14	2:21
July 7 – August 7	Yin Fire	Sheep	Yang Water	Dragon	July	44	12:45
August 7 – September 8	Yang Earth	Monkey	Yang Water	Dragon	Aug	15	22:32
September 8 – October 8	Yin Earth	Cock	Yang Water	Dragon	Sep	46	1:14
October 8 – November 7	Yang Metal	Dog	Yang Water	Dragon	Oct	16	16:33
November 7 – December 7	Yin Metal	Pig	Yang Water	Dragon	Nov	47	19:22
December 7 – January 6	Yang Water	Rat	Yang Water	Dragon	Dec	17	11:56

1953

	Month		Year				
Find your Day Here	Stem	Branch	Stem	Branch	Day	Day	Time
January 5- February 4	Yin Water	Ox	Yang Water	Dragon	Jan	48	23: 03
February 4 – March 6	Yang Wood	Tiger	Yin Water	Snake	Feb	19	10: 46
March 6 – April 5	Yin Wood	Rabbit	Yin Water	Snake	Mar	47	4: 56
April 5 – May 6	Yang Fire	Dragon	Yin Water	Snake	April	18	5: 03
May 6 – June 6	Yin Fire	Snake	Yin Water	Snake	May	48	3: 53
June 6 – July 8	Yang Earth	Horse	Yin Water	Snake	June	19	8: 17
July 8 – August 8	Yin Earth	Sheep	Yin Water	Snake	July	49	18:36
August 8 – September 8	Yang Metal	Monkey	Yin Water	Snake	Aug	20	4: 15
September 8 – October 8	Yin Metal	Cock	Yin Water	Snake	Sep	51	6: 54
October 8 – November 8	Yang Water	Dog	Yin Water	Snake	Oct	21	22: 11
November 8 – December 7	Yin Water	Pig	Yin Water	Snake	Nov	52	1: 02
December 7 – January 6	Yang Wood	Rat	Yin Water	Snake	Dec	22	17: 38

Branch	Pig	Rat	Ox	Tiger	Rabbit	Dragon	Snake	Horse	Sheep	Monkey	Cock	Dog
Main Element	Yang Water	Yin Water	Yin Earth	Yang Wood	Yin Wood	Yang Earth	Yang Fire	Yang Fire	Yin Earth	Yang Metal	Yin Metal	Yang Earth
Hidden Elements	Yang Wood		Yin Water	Yang Fire		Yin Wood	Yang Earth	Yin Earth	Yin Fire	Yang Earth		Yin Metal
			Yin Metal	Yang Earth		Yin Water	Yang Metal		Yin Wood	Yang Water		Yin Fire

1954

Find your Day Here	Month Stem	Branch	Year Stem	Branch	Day	Day	Time
January 6- February 4	Yin Wood	Ox	Yin Water	Snake	Jan	53	4:46
February 4 – March 6	Yang Fire	Tiger	Yang Wood	Horse	Feb	24	16:31
March 6 – April 5	Yin Fire	Rabbit	Yang Wood	Horse	Mar	52	10:49
April 5 – May 6	Yang Earth	Dragon	Yang Wood	Horse	April	23	16:00
May 6 – June 6	Yin Earth	Snake	Yang Wood	Horse	May	53	9:39
June 6 – July 8	Yang Metal	Horse	Yang Wood	Horse	June	24	14:02
July 8 – August 8	Yin Metal	Sheep	Yang Wood	Horse	July	54	:20
August 8 – September 8	Yang Water	Monkey	Yang Wood	Horse	Aug	25	10:00
September 8 – October 9	Yin Water	Cock	Yang Wood	Horse	Sep	56	12:39
October 9 – November 8	Yang Wood	Dog	Yang Wood	Horse	Oct	26	3:58
November 8 – December 8	Yin Wood	Pig	Yang Wood	Horse	Nov	57	6:51
December 8 – January 6	Yang Fire	Rat	Yang Wood	Horse	Dec	27	23:29

1955

Find your Day Here	Month Stem	Branch	Year Stem	Branch	Day	Day	Time
January 6- February 4	Yin Fire	Ox	Yang Wood	Horse	Jan	58	10: 36
February 4 – March 6	Yang Earth	Tiger	Yin Wood	Sheep	Feb	29	22: 18
March 6 – April 5	Yin Earth	Rabbit	Yin Wood	Sheep	Mar	57	16: 32
April 5 – May 6	Yang Metal	Dragon	Yin Wood	Sheep	April	28	21: 39
May 6 – June 6	Yin Metal	Snake	Yin Wood	Sheep	May	58	15: 18
June 6 – July 8	Yang Water	Horse	Yin Wood	Sheep	June	29	19: 44
July 8 – August 8	Yin Water	Sheep	Yin Wood	Sheep	July	59	6: 07
August 8 – September 8	Yang Wood	Monkey	Yin Wood	Sheep	Aug	30	15: 50
September 8 – October 9	Yin Wood	Cock	Yin Wood	Sheep	Sep	1	18: 32
October 9 – November 8	Yang Fire	Dog	Yin Wood	Sheep	Oct	31	9: 53
November 8 – December 8	Yin Fire	Pig	Yin Wood	Sheep	Nov	2	12: 46
December 8 – January 6	Yang Earth	Rat	Yin Wood	Sheep	Dec	32	5: 23

Branch	Pig	Rat	Ox	Tiger	Rabbit	Dragon	Snake	Horse	Sheep	Monkey	Cock	Dog
Main Element	Yang Water	Yin Water	Yin Earth	Yang Wood	Yin Wood	Yang Earth	Yang Fire	Yin Fire	Yin Earth	Yang Metal	Yin Metal	Yang Earth
Hidden Elements	Yang Wood		Yin Water	Yang Fire		Yin Wood	Yang Earth	Yin Earth	Yin Fire	Yang Earth		Yin Metal
			Yin Metal	Yang Earth		Yin Water	Yang Metal		Yin Wood	Yang Water		Yin Fire

1956

	Month		Year				
Find your Day Here	Stem	Branch	Stem	Branch	Day	Day	Time
January 6 – February 5	Yin Earth	Ox	Yin Wood	Sheep	Jan	3	16: 31
February 5 – 29, March 5	Yang Metal	Tiger	Yang Fire	Monkey	Feb	34	4: 12
March 5 – April 5	Yin Metal	Rabbit	Yang Fire	Monkey	Mar	3	22: 25
April 5 – May 5	Yang Water	Dragon	Yang Fire	Monkey	April	34	3: 32
May 5 – June 6	Yin Water	Snake	Yang Fire	Monkey	May	4	21: 11
June 6 – July 7	Yang Wood	Horse	Yang Fire	Monkey	June	35	1: 36
July 7 – August 7	Yin Wood	Sheep	Yang Fire	Monkey	July	5	11: 59
August 7 – September 8	Yang Fire	Monkey	Yang Fire	Monkey	Aug	36	9: 41
September 8 – October 8	Yin Fire	Cock	Yang Fire	Monkey	Sep	7	: 20
October 8 – November 7	Yang Earth	Dog	Yang Fire	Monkey	Oct	37	15: 37
November 7 – December 7	Yin Earth	Pig	Yang Fire	Monkey	Nov	8	18: 27
December 7 – January 5	Yang Metal	Rat	Yang Fire	Monkey	Dec	38	11: 03

1957

	Month		Year				
Find your Day Here	Stem	Branch	Stem	Branch	Day	Day	Time
January 5 – February 4	Yin Metal	Ox	Yang Fire	Monkey	Jan	4	22: 11
February 4— March 6	Yang Water	Tiger	Yin Fire	Cock	Feb	40	9: 55
March 6— April 5	Yin Water	Rabbit	Yin Fire	Cock	Mar	8	4: 11
April 5— May 6	Yang Wood	Dragon	Yin Fire	Cock	April	39	9: 19
May 6—June 6	Yin Wood	Snake	Yin Fire	Cock	May	9	2: 59
June 6— July 7	Yang Fire	Horse	Yin Fire	Cock	June	40	7: 25
July 7— August 8	Yin Fire	Sheep	Yin Fire	Cock	July	10	17: 49
August 8— September 8	Yang Earth	Monkey	Yin Fire	Cock	Aug	41	3: 33
September 8—October 8	Yin Earth	Cock	Yin Fire	Cock	Sep	12	6: 13
October 8— November 8	Yang Metal	Dog	Yin Fire	Cock	Oct	42	21: 31
November 8— December 7	Yin Metal	Pig	Yin Fire	Cock	Nov	13	12: 21
December 7—January 6	Yang Water	Rat	Yin Fire	Cock	Dec	43	16:57

Branch	Pig	Rat	Ox	Tiger	Rabbit	Dragon	Snake	Horse	Sheep	Monkey	Cock	Dog
Main Element	Yang Water	Yin Water	Yin Earth	Yang Wood	Yin Wood	Yang Earth	Yang Fire	Yin Fire	Yin Earth	Yang Metal	Yin Metal	Yang Earth
Hidden Elements	Yang Wood		Yin Water	Yang Fire		Yin Wood	Yang Earth	Yin Earth	Yin Fire	Yang Earth		Yin Metal
			Yin Metal	Yang Earth		Yin Water	Yang Metal		Yin Wood	Yang Water		Yin Fire

1958

Find your Day Here	Month Stem	Branch	Year Stem	Branch	Day	Day	Time
January 6—February 4	Yin Water	Ox	Yin Fire	Cock	Jan	14	4: 05
February 4 – March 6	Yang Wood	Tiger	Yang Earth	Dog	Feb	45	15: 49
March 6 – April 5	Yin Wood	Rabbit	Yang Earth	Dog	Mar	13	10: 06
April 5 – May 6	Yang Fire	Dragon	Yang Earth	Dog	April	44	15: 13
May 6 – June 6	Yin Fire	Snake	Yang Earth	Dog	May	14	8: 50
June 6 – July 8	Yang Earth	Horse	Yang Earth	Dog	June	45	13: 13
July 8 – August 8	Yin Earth	Sheep	Yang Earth	Dog	July	15	23: 34
August 8 – September 8	Yang Metal	Monkey	Yang Earth	Dog	Aug	46	9: 18
September 8 – October 9	Yin Metal	Cock	Yang Earth	Dog	Sep	17	12: 00
October 9 – November 8	Yang Water	Dog	Yang Earth	Dog	Oct	47	3: 20
November 8 – December 7	Yin Water	Pig	Yang Earth	Dog	Nov	18	6: 13
December 7 – January 6	Yang Wood	Rat	Yang Earth	Dog	Dec	48	22: 50

1959

Find your Day Here	Month Stem	Branch	Year Stem	Branch	Day	Day	Time
January 6 – February 4	Yin Wood	Ox	Yang Earth	Dog	Jan	19	9: 59
February 4— March 6	Yang Fire	Tiger	Yin Earth	Pig	Feb	50	21: 423
March 6— April 5	Yin Fire	Rabbit	Yin Earth	Pig	Mar	18	15: 57
April 5— May 6	Yang Earth	Dragon	Yin Earth	Pig	April	49	21: 04
May 6 – June 6	Yin Earth	Snake	Yin Earth	Pig	May	19	14: 39
June 6— July 8	Yang Metal	Horse	Yin Earth	Pig	June	50	19: 01
July 8— August 8	Yin Metal	Sheep	Yin Earth	Pig	July	20	5: 21
August 8— September 8	Yang Water	Monkey	Yin Earth	Pig	Aug	51	15: 05
September 8—October 8	Yin Water	Cock	Yin Earth	Pig	Sep	22	17: 49
October 9— November 8	Yang Wood	Dog	Yin Earth	Pig	Oct	52	9: 11
November 8— December 8	Yin Wood	Pig	Yin Earth	Pig	Nov	23	12: 03
December 8—January 6	Yang Fire	Rat	Yin Earth	Pig	Dec	53	4: 38

Branch	Pig	Rat	Ox	Tiger	Rabbit	Dragon	Snake	Horse	Sheep	Monkey	Cock	Dog
Main Element	Yang Water	Yin Water	Yin Earth	Yang Wood	Yin Wood	Yang Earth	Yang Fire	Yin Fire	Yin Earth	Yang Metal	Yin Metal	Yang Earth
Hidden Elements	Yang Wood		Yin Water	Yang Fire		Yin Wood	Yang Earth	Yin Earth	Yin Fire	Yang Earth		Yin Metal
			Yin Metal	Yang Earth		Yin Water	Yang Metal		Yin Wood	Yang Water		Yin Fire

1960

	Month		Year				
Find your Day Here	Stem	Branch	Stem	Branch	Day	Day	Time
January 6 – February 5	Yin Fire	Ox	Yin Earth	Pig	Jan	24	15: 43
February 5 –29, March 5	Yang Earth	Tiger	Yang Metal	Rat	Feb	55	3: 24
March 5— April 5	Yin Earth	Rabbit	Yang Metal	Rat	Mar	24	21: 36
April 5— May 5	Yang Metal	Dragon	Yang Metal	Rat	April	55	2: 44
May 5—June 6	Yin Metal	Snake	Yang Metal	Rat	May	25	20: 23
June 6— July 7	Yang Water	Horse	Yang Metal	Rat	June	56	: 49
July 7— August 7	Yin Water	Sheep	Yang Metal	Rat	July	26	11: 13
August 7— September 8	Yang Wood	Monkey	Yang Metal	Rat	Aug	57	21: 00
September 8—October 8	Yin Wood	Cock	Yang Metal	Rat	Sep	28	23: 46
October 8— November 7	Yang Fire	Dog	Yang Metal	Rat	Oct	58	15: 09
November 7— December 7	Yin Fire	Pig	Yang Metal	Rat	Nov	29	18: 02
December 7—January 5	Yang Earth	Rat	Yang Metal	Rat	Dec	59	10:38

1961

	Month		Year				
Find your Day Here	Stem	Branch	Stem	Branch	Day	Day	Time
January 5 – February 4	Yin Earth	Ox	Yang Metal	Rat	Jan	30	21: 43
February 4— March 6	Yang Metal	Tiger	Yin Metal	Ox	Feb	1	9: 22
March 6— April 5	Yin Metal	Rabbit	Yin Metal	Ox	Mar	29	3: 35
April 5— May 6	Yang Water	Dragon	Yin Metal	Ox	April	60	8: 42
May 6—June 6	Yin Water	Snake	Yin Metal	Ox	May	30	2: 21
June 6— July 7	Yang Wood	Horse	Yin Metal	Ox	June	1	6: 46
July 7— August 8	Yin Wood	Sheep	Yin Metal	Ox	July	31	17: 07
August 8— September 8	Yang Fire	Monkey	Yin Metal	Ox	Aug	2	2: 49
September 8—October 8	Yin Fire	Cock	Yin Metal	Ox	Sep	33	5: 29
October 8— November 8	Yang Earth	Dog	Yin Metal	Ox	Oct	3	20: 51
November 8— December 7	Yin Earth	Pig	Yin Metal	Ox	Nov	34	23: 46
December 7—January 6	Yang Metal	Rat	Yin Metal	Ox	Dec	4	16: 26

Branch	Pig	Rat	Ox	Tiger	Rabbit	Dragon	Snake	Horse	Sheep	Monkey	Cock	Dog
Main Element	Yang Water	Yin Water	Yin Earth	Yang Wood	Yin Wood	Yang Earth	Yang Fire	Yin Fire	Yin Earth	Yang Metal	Yin Metal	Yang Earth
Hidden Elements	Yang Wood		Yin Water / Yin Metal	Yang Fire / Yang Earth		Yin Wood / Yin Water	Yang Earth / Yang Metal	Yin Earth	Yin Fire / Yin Wood	Yang Earth / Yang Water		Yin Metal / Yin Fire

1962

Find your Day Here	Month Stem	Branch	Year Stem	Branch	Day	Day	Time
January 6 – February 4	Yin Metal	Ox	Yin Metal	Ox	Jan	35	3: 35
February 4— March 6	Yang Water	Tiger	Yang Water	Tiger	Feb	6	15: 18
March 6— April 5	Yin Water	Rabbit	Yang Water	Tiger	Mar	6	9: 30
April 5— May 6	Yang Wood	Dragon	Yang Water	Tiger	April	6	14: 34
May 6 – June 6	Yin Wood	Snake	Yang Water	Tiger	May	35	8: 10
June 6— July 7	Yang Fire	Horse	Yang Water	Tiger	June	6	12: 31
July 7— August 8	Yin Fire	Sheep	Yang Water	Tiger	July	36	22: 51
August 8— September 8	Yang Earth	Monkey	Yang Water	Tiger	Aug	7	8: 34
September 8—October 9	Yin Earth	Cock	Yang Water	Tiger	Sep	38	11: 16
October 9— November 8	Yang Metal	Dog	Yang Water	Tiger	Oct	8	2: 38
November 8— December 7	Yin Metal	Pig	Yang Water	Tiger	Nov	39	5: 35
December 7—January 6	Yang Water	Rat	Yang Water	Tiger	Dec	9	22: 17

1963

Find your Day Here	Month Stem	Branch	Year Stem	Branch	Day	Day	Time
January 6 – February 4	Yin Water	Ox	Yang Water	Tiger	Jan	40	9: 27
February 4— March 6	Yang Wood	Tiger	Yin Water	Rabbit	Feb	11	21: 08
March 6— April 5	Yin Wood	Rabbit	Yin Water	Rabbit	Mar	39	15: 17
April 5— May 6	Yang Fire	Dragon	Yin Water	Rabbit	April	10	20: 19
May 6 – June 6	Yin Fire	Snake	Yin Water	Rabbit	May	40	13: 52
June 6— July 7	Yang Earth	Horse	Yin Water	Rabbit	June	11	18: 15
July 8— August 8	Yin Earth	Sheep	Yin Water	Rabbit	July	41	4: 38
August 8— September 8	Yang Metal	Monkey	Yin Water	Rabbit	Aug	12	14: 26
September 8 – October 9	Yin Metal	Cock	Yin Water	Rabbit	Sep	43	17: 12
October 9— November 8	Yang Water	Dog	Yin Water	Rabbit	Oct	13	8: 36
November 8— December 8	Yin Water	Pig	Yin Water	Rabbit	Nov	44	11: 32
December 8—January 6	Yang Wood	Rat	Yin Water	Rabbit	Dec	14	4: 13

Branch	Pig	Rat	Ox	Tiger	Rabbit	Dragon	Snake	Horse	Sheep	Monkey	Cock	Dog
Main Element	Yang Water	Yin Water	Yin Earth	Yang Wood	Yin Wood	Yang Earth	Yang Fire	Yin Fire	Yin Earth	Yang Metal	Yin Metal	Yang Earth
Hidden Elements	Yang Wood		Yin Water	Yang Fire		Yin Wood	Yang Earth	Yin Earth	Yin Fire	Yang Earth		Yin Metal
			Yin Metal	Yang Earth		Yin Water	Yang Metal		Yin Wood	Yang Water		Yin Fire

1964

| | Month | | Year | | | | |
Find your Day Here	Stem	Branch	Stem	Branch	Day	Day	Time
January 6- February 5	Yin Wood	Ox	Yin Water	Rabbit	Jan	45	15: 22
February 5-29,— March 5	Yang Fire	Tiger	Yang Wood	Dragon	Feb	16	3: 05
March 5 – April 5	Yin Fire	Rabbit	Yang Wood	Dragon	Mar	45	21: 16
April 5 – May 5	Yang Earth	Dragon	Yang Wood	Dragon	April	16	2: 18
May 5 – June 6	Yin Earth	Snake	Yang Wood	Dragon	May	46	19: 51
June 6 – July 7	Yang Metal	Horse	Yang Wood	Dragon	June	17	: 12
July 7 – August 7	Yin Metal	Sheep	Yang Wood	Dragon	July	47	10: 32
August 7 – September 7	Yang Water	Monkey	Yang Wood	Dragon	Aug	18	20: 16
September 7 – October 8	Yin Water	Cock	Yang Wood	Dragon	Sep	49	23:00
October 8 – November 7	Yang Wood	Dog	Yang Wood	Dragon	Oct	19	14: 22
November 7 – December 7	Yin Wood	Pig	Yang Wood	Dragon	Nov	50	17: 15
December 7 – January 5	Yang Fire	Rat	Yang Wood	Dragon	Dec	20	9: 53

1965

| | Month | | Year | | | | |
Find your Day Here	Stem	Branch	Stem	Branch	Day	Day	Time
January 5 – February 4	Yin Fire	Ox	Yang Wood	Dragon	Jan	51	21: 02
February 4— March 6	Yang Earth	Tiger	Yin Wood	Snake	Feb	27	8: 46
March 6— April 5	Yin Earth	Rabbit	Yin Wood	Snake	Mar	50	3: 01
April 5— May 6	Yang Metal	Dragon	Yin Wood	Snake	April	21	8: 07
May 6—June 6	Yin Metal	Snake	Yin Wood	Snake	May	51	1: 42
June 6— July 7	Yang Water	Horse	Yin Wood	Snake	June	22	6: 02
July 7— August 8	Yin Water	Sheep	Yin Wood	Snake	July	52	16: 22
August 8— September 8	Yang Wood	Monkey	Yin Wood	Snake	Aug	23	2: 05
September 8 – October 8	Yin Wood	Cock	Yin Wood	Snake	Sep	54	4: 48
October 8— November 7	Yang Fire	Dog	Yin Wood	Snake	Oct	24	20: 11
November 7— December 7	Yin Fire	Pig	Yin Wood	Snake	Nov	55	23: 07
December 7—January 6	Yang Earth	Rat	Yin Wood	Snake	Dec	25	15: 46

Branch	Pig	Rat	Ox	Tiger	Rabbit	Dragon	Snake	Horse	Sheep	Monkey	Cock	Dog
Main Element	Yang Water	Yin Water	Yin Earth	Yang Wood	Yin Wood	Yang Earth	Yang Fire	Yin Fire	Yin Earth	Yang Metal	Yin Metal	Yang Earth
Hidden Elements	Yang Wood		Yin Water	Yang Fire		Yin Wood	Yang Earth	Yin Earth	Yin Fire	Yang Earth		Yin Metal
			Yin Metal	Yang Earth		Yin Water	Yang Metal		Yin Wood	Yang Water		Yin Fire

1966

Find your Day Here	Month Stem	Branch	Year Stem	Branch	Day	Day	Time
January 6 – February 4	Yin Earth	Ox	Yin Wood	Snake	Jan	56	2: 55
February 4 – 29, March 6	Yang Metal	Tiger	Yang Fire	Horse	Feb	27	14: 38
March 6 – April 5	Yin Metal	Rabbit	Yang Fire	Horse	Mar	55	8: 51
April 5 – May 6	Yang Water	Dragon	Yang Fire	Horse	April	26	13: 57
May 6 – June 6	Yin Water	Snake	Yang Fire	Horse	May	56	7: 31
June 6 – July 7	Yang Wood	Horse	Yang Fire	Horse	June	27	11: 50
July 7 – August 8	Yin Wood	Sheep	Yang Fire	Horse	July	57	22: 07
August 8– September 8	Yang Fire	Monkey	Yang Fire	Horse	Aug	28	7: 49
September 8 – October 9	Yin Fire	Cock	Yang Fire	Horse	Sep	59	10: 32
October 9 – November 8	Yang Earth	Dog	Yang Fire	Horse	Oct	29	1: 57
November 8 – December 7	Yin Earth	Pig	Yang Fire	Horse	Nov	60	4: 56
December 7 – January 6	Yang Metal	Rat	Yang Fire	Horse	Dec	30	21: 38

1967

Find your Day Here	Month Stem	Branch	Year Stem	Branch	Day	Day	Time
January 6 – February 4	Yin Metal	Ox	Yang Fire	Horse	Jan	1	8: 48
February 4— March 6	Yang Water	Tiger	Yin Fire	Sheep	Feb	32	20: 31
March 6— April 5	Yin Water	Rabbit	Yin Fire	Sheep	Mar	60	14: 42
April 5— May 6	Yang Wood	Dragon	Yin Fire	Sheep	April	31	19: 45
May 6 – June 6	Yin Wood	Snake	Yin Fire	Sheep	May	1	13: 18
June 6— July 8	Yang Fire	Horse	Yin Fire	Sheep	June	32	17: 36
July 8— August 8	Yin Fire	Sheep	Yin Fire	Sheep	July	2	3: 54
August 8— September 8	Yang Earth	Monkey	Yin Fire	Sheep	Aug	33	13: 35
September 8 – October 9	Yin Earth	Cock	Yin Fire	Sheep	Sep	4	16: 18
October 9— November 8	Yang Metal	Dog	Yin Fire	Sheep	Oct	34	7: 42
November 8— December 8	Yin Metal	Pig	Yin Fire	Sheep	Nov	5	10: 32
December 8—January 6	Yang Water	Rat	Yin Fire	Sheep	Dec	35	3: 18

Branch	Pig	Rat	Ox	Tiger	Rabbit	Dragon	Snake	Horse	Sheep	Monkey	Cock	Dog
Main Element	Yang Water	Yin Water	Yin Earth	Yang Wood	Yin Wood	Yang Earth	Yang Fire	Yin Fire	Yin Earth	Yang Metal	Yin Metal	Yang Earth
Hidden Elements	Yang Wood		Yin Water	Yang Fire		Yin Wood	Yang Earth	Yin Earth	Yin Fire	Yang Earth		Yin Metal
			Yin Metal	Yang Earth		Yin Water	Yang Metal		Yin Wood	Yang Water		Yin Fire

1968

	Month		Year				
Find your Day Here	Stem	Branch	Stem	Branch	Day	Day	Time
January 6 – February 5	Yin Water	Ox	Yin Fire	Sheep	Jan	6	14: 26
February 5 – 29,— March 5	Yang Wood	Tiger	Yang Earth	Monkey	Feb	37	2: 08
March 5— April 5	Yin Wood	Rabbit	Yang Earth	Monkey	Mar	6	20: 18
April 5— May 5	Yang Fire	Dragon	Yang Earth	Monkey	April	37	1: 21
May 5 – June 6	Yin Fire	Snake	Yang Earth	Monkey	May	7	18: 56
June 6— July 7	Yang Earth	Horse	Yang Earth	Monkey	June	38	23: 19
July 7— August 7	Yin Earth	Sheep ·	Yang Earth	Monkey	July	8	9: 42
August 7— September 7	Yang Metal	Monkey	Yang Earth	Monkey	Aug	39	19: 27
September 7 – October 8	Yin Metal	Cock	Yang Earth	Monkey	Sep	10	22: 12
October 8— November 7	Yang Water	Dog	Yang Earth	Monkey	Oct	40	13: 35
November 7— December 7	Yin Water	Pig	Yang Earth	Monkey	Nov	11	16: 29
December 7—January 5	Yang Wood	Rat	Yang Earth	Monkey	Dec	41	9: 09

1969

	Month		Year				
Find your Day Here	Stem	Branch	Stem	Branch	Day	Day	Time
January 5 – February 4	Yin Wood	Ox	Yang Earth Monkey		Jan	12	20: 17
February 4— March 6	Yang Fire	Tiger	Yin Earth	Cock	Feb	43	7: 59
March 6— April 5	Yin Fire	Rabbit	Yin Earth	Cock	Mar	11	2: 11
April 5— May 6	Yang Earth	Dragon	Yin Earth	Cock	April	42	7: 15
May 6 – June 6	Yin Earth	Snake	Yin Earth	Cock	May	12	: 50
June 6— July 7	Yang Metal	Horse	Yin Earth	Cock	June	43	5: 12
July 7— August 8	Yin Metal	Sheep	Yin Earth	Cock	July	13	15: 32
August 8— September 8	Yang Water	Monkey	Yin Earth	Cock	Aug	44	1: 14
September 8 – October 8	Yin Water	Cock	Yin Earth	Cock	Sep	15	3: 56
October 8— November 7	Yang Wood	Dog	Yin Earth	Cock	Oct	45	19: 17
November 7— December 7	Yin Wood	Pig	Yin Earth	Cock	Nov	16	22: 12
December 7—January 6	Yang Fire	Rat	Yin Earth	Cock	Dec	46	14: 51

Branch	Pig	Rat	Ox	Tiger	Rabbit	Dragon	Snake	Horse	Sheep	Monkey	Cock	Dog
Main Element	Yang Water	Yin Water	Yin Earth	Yang Wood	Yin Wood	Yang Earth	Yang Fire	Yin Fire	Yin Earth	Yang Metal	Yin Metal	Yang Earth
Hidden Elements	Yang Wood		Yin Water	Yang Fire		Yin Wood	Yang Earth	Yin Earth	Yin Fire	Yang Earth		Yin Metal
			Yin Metal	Yang Earth		Yin Water	Yang Metal		Yin Wood	Yang Water		Yin Fire

1970

Find your Day Here	Month Stem	Branch	Year Stem	Branch	Day	Day	Time
January 6 – February 4	Yin Fire	Ox	Yin Earth	Cock	Jan	17	1:59
February 4— March 6	Yang Earth	Tiger	Yang Metal	Dog	Feb	48	13:46
March 6— April 5	Yin Earth	Rabbit	Yang Metal	Dog	Mar	16	7:51
April 5— May 6	Yang Metal	Dragon	Yang Metal	Dog	April	47	12:54
May 6 – June 6	Yin Metal	Snake	Yang Metal	Dog	May	17	6:28
June 6— July 7	Yang Water	Horse	Yang Metal	Dog	June	48	10:51
July 7— August 8	Yin Water	Sheep	Yang Metal	Dog	July	18	21:14
August 8— September 8	Yang Wood	Monkey	Yang Metal	Dog	Aug	49	6:58
September 8 – October 9	Yin Wood	Cock	Yang Metal	Dog	Sep	20	9:42
October 9— November 8	Yang Fire	Dog	Yang Metal	Dog	Oct	50	1:06
November 8— December 7	Yin Fire	Pig	Yang Metal	Dog	Nov	21	4:01
December 7—January 6	Yang Earth	Rat	Yang Metal	Dog	Dec	51	21:41

1971

Find your Day Here	Month Stem	Branch	Year Stem	Branch	Day	Day	Time
January 6 – February 4	Yin Earth	Ox	Yang Metal	Dog	Jan	22	7: 45
February 4 – 29, March 6	Yang Metal	Tiger	Yin Metal	Pig	Feb	53	19 :26
March 6 – April 5	Yin Metal	Rabbit	Yin Metal	Pig	Mar	21	13: 35
April 5 – May 6	Yang Water	Dragon	Yin Metal	Pig	April	52	18: 36
May 6 – June 6	Yin Water	Snake	Yin Metal	Pig	May	22	12: 08
June 6 – July 8	Yang Wood	Horse	Yin Metal	Pig	June	53	16: 29
July 8 – August 8	Yin Wood	Sheep	Yin Metal	Pig	July	23	2:51
August 8– September 8	Yang Fire	Monkey	Yin Metal	Pig	Aug	54	12: 40
September 8 – October 9	Yin Fire	Cock	Yin Metal	Pig	Sep	25	17: 30
October 9 – November 8	Yang Earth	Dog	Yin Metal	Pig	Oct	55	6: 59
November 8 – December 8	Yin Earth	Pig	Yin Metal	Pig	Nov	26	9:5
December 8 – January 6	Yang Metal	Rat	Yin Metal	Pig	Dec	56	2:36

Branch	Pig	Rat	Ox	Tiger	Rabbit	Dragon	Snake	Horse	Sheep	Monkey	Cock	Dog
Main Element	Yang Water	Yin Water	Yin Earth	Yang Wood	Yin Wood	Yang Earth	Yang Fire	Yin Fire	Yin Earth	Yang Metal	Yin Metal	Yang Earth
Hidden Elements	Yang Wood		Yin Water	Yang Fire		Yin Wood	Yang Earth	Yin Earth	Yin Fire	Yang Earth		Yin Metal
			Yin Metal	Yang Earth		Yin Water	Yang Metal		Yin Wood	Yang Water		Yin Fire

1972

Find your Day Here	Month Stem	Branch	Year Stem	Branch	Day	Day	Time
January 6 – February 5	Yin Metal	Ox	Yin Metal	Pig	Jan	27	13: 43
February 5 – 29,— March 5	Yang Water	Tiger	Yang Water	Rat	Feb	58	1320
March 5— April 5	Yin Water	Rabbit	Yang Water	Rat	Mar	27	19: 28
April 5— May 5	Yang Wood	Dragon	Yang Water	Rat	April	58	12:29
May 5 – June 5	Yin Wood	Snake	Yang Water	Rat	May	59	18: 16
June 5— July 7	Yang Fire	Horse	Yang Water	Rat	June	59	22: 22
July 7— August 7	Yin Fire	Sheep	Yang Water	Rat	July	29	8:43
August 7— September 7	Yang Earth	Monkey	Yang Water	Rat	Aug	31	18:29
September 7 – October 8	Yin Earth	Cock	Yang Water	Rat	Sep	31	21: 15
October 8— November 7	Yang Metal	Dog	Yang Water	Rat	Oct	1	14: 42
November 7— December 7	Yin Metal	Pig	Yang Water	Rat	Nov	32	15: 40
December 7—January 5	Yang Water	Rat	Yang Water	Rat	Dec	2	8:19

1973

Find your Day Here	Month Stem	Branch	Year Stem	Branch	Day	Day	Time
January 5 – February 4	Yin Water	Ox	Yang Water	Rat	Jan	33	19: 26
February 4— March 6	Yang Wood	Tiger	Yin Water	Ox	Feb	4	7: 04
March 6— April 5	Yin Wood	Rabbit	Yin Water	Ox	Mar	32	1: 13
April 5— May 6	Yang Fire	Dragon	Yin Water	Ox	April	3	6: 14
May 6 – June 6	Yin Fire	Snake	Yin Water	Ox	May	33	23:47
June 6— July 7	Yang Earth	Horse	Yin Water	Ox	June	4	4: 07
July 7— August 8	Yin Earth	Sheep	Yin Water	Ox	July	34	14:28
August 8— September 8	Yang Metal	Monkey	Yin Water	Ox	Aug	5	:13
September 8 – October 8	Yin Metal	Cock	Yin Water	Ox	Sep	36	3: 00
October 8— November 7	Yang Water	Dog	Yin Water	Ox	Oct	6	18:27
November 7— December 7	Yin Water	Pig	Yin Water	Ox	Nov	37	21: 28
December 7 – January 6	Yang Wood	Rat	Yin Water	Ox	Dec	7	14 :11

Branch	Pig	Rat	Ox	Tiger	Rabbit	Dragon	Snake	Horse	Sheep	Monkey	Cock	Dog
Main Element	Yang Water	Yin Water	Yin Earth	Yang Wood	Yin Wood	Yang Earth	Yang Fire	Yang Fire	Yin Earth	Yang Metal	Yin Metal	Yang Earth
Hidden Elements	Yang Wood		Yin Water / Yin Metal	Yang Fire / Yang Earth		Yin Wood / Yin Water	Yang Earth / Yang Metal	Yin Earth	Yin Fire / Yin Wood	Yang Earth / Yang Water		Yin Metal / Yin Fire

1974

	Month		Year				
Find your Day Here	Stem	Branch	Stem	Branch	Day	Day	Time
January 6 – February 4	Yin Wood	Ox	Yin Water	Ox	Jan	38	1: 20
February 4— March 6	Yang Fire	Tiger	Yang Wood	Tiger	Feb	9	13: 00
March 6— April 5	Yin Fire	Rabbit	Yang Wood	Tiger	Mar	37	7: 07
April 5— May 6	Yang Earth	Dragon	Yang Wood	Tiger	April	8	12: 05
May 6 – June 6	Yin Earth	Snake	Yang Wood	Tiger	May	38	5: 34
June 6— July 7	Yang Metal	Horse	Yang Wood	Tiger	June	9	9: 52
July 7— August 8	Yin Metal	Sheep	Yang Wood	Tiger	July	39	20: 13
August 8— September 8	Yang Water	Monkey	Yang Wood	Tiger	Aug	10	5: 57
September 8 – October 9	Yin Water	Cock	Yang Wood	Tiger	Sep	41	8:45
October 9— November 8	Yang Wood	Dog	Yang Wood	Tiger	Oct	11	: 15
November 8— December 7	Yin Wood	Pig	Yang Wood	Tiger	Nov	42	3: 18
December 7 – January 6	Yang Fire	Rat	Yang Wood	Tiger	Dec	12	20:05

1975

	Month		Year				
Find your Day Here	Stem	Branch	Stem	Branch	Day	Day	Time
January 6 – February 4	Yin Fire	Ox	Yang Wood	Monkey	Jan	6	:35
February 4— March 6	Yang Earth	Tiger	Yin Wood	Cock	Feb	37	12:20
March 6—April 5	Yin Earth	Rabbit	Yin Wood	Cock	Mar	5	6:38
April 5— May 6	Yang Metal	Dragon	Yin Wood	Cock	April	36	11:52
May 6 – June 6	Yin Metal	Snake	Yin Wood	Cock	May	6	5:37
June 6 – July 7	Yang Water	Horse	Yin Wood	Cock	June	37	10:06
July 7— August 8	Yin Water	Sheep	Yin Wood	Cock	July	7	20:27
August 8—September 8	Yang Wood	Monkey	Yin Wood	Cock	Aug	38	6:06
September 8— October 9	Yin Wood	Cock	Yin Wood	Cock	Sep	9	8:39
October 9— November 8	Yang Fire	Dog	Yin Wood	Cock	Oct	39	23:50
November 8—December 7	Yin Fire	Pig	Yin Wood	Cock	Nov	10	2:35
December 7— January 6	Yang Earth	Rat	Yin Wood	Cock	Dec	40	19:08

Branch	Pig	Rat	Ox	Tiger	Rabbit	Dragon	Snake	Horse	Sheep	Monkey	Cock	Dog
Main Element	Yang Water	Yin Water	Yin Earth	Yang Wood	Yin Wood	Yang Earth	Yang Fire	Yin Fire	Yin Earth	Yang Metal	Yin Metal	Yang Earth
Hidden Elements	Yang Wood		Yin Water	Yang Fire		Yin Wood	Yang Earth	Yin Earth	Yin Fire	Yang Earth		Yin Metal
			Yin Metal	Yang Earth		Yin Water	Yang Metal		Yin Wood	Yang Water		Yin Fire

1976

| | **Month** | | **Year** | | | | |
Find your Day Here	Stem	Branch	Stem	Branch	Day	Day	Time
January 6 – February 5	Yin Earth	Ox	Yin Wood	Rabbit	Jan	48	12: 58
February 5— 29,—March 5	Yang Metal	Tiger	Yang Fire	Dragon	Feb	19	: 40
March 5— April 5	Yin Metal	Rabbit	Yang Fire	Dragon	Mar	48	18: 48
April 5— May 5	Yang Water	Dragon	Yang Fire	Dragon	April	19	23: 47
May 5 – June 5	Yin Water	Snake	Yang Fire	Dragon	May	49	17: 15
June 5— July 7	Yang Wood	Horse	Yang Fire	Dragon	June	20	21:31
July 7— August 7	Yin Wood	Sheep	Yang Fire	Dragon	July	50	7: 51
August 7— September 7	Yang Fire	Monkey	Yang Fire	Dragon	Aug	21	17: 39
September 7 – October 8	Yin Fire	Cock	Yang Fire	Dragon	Sep	52	20:28
October 8— November 7	Yang Earth	Dog	Yang Fire	Dragon	Oct	22	11: 58
November 7— December 7	Yin Earth	Pig	Yang Fire	Dragon	Nov	53	14: 59
December 7—January 5	Yang Metal	Rat	Yang Fire	Dragon	Dec	23	7: 41

1977

| | **Month** | | **Year** | | | | |
Find your Day Here	Stem	Branch	Stem	Branch	Day	Day	Time
January 5 – February 4	Yin Metal	Ox	Yang Fire	Dragon	Jan	54	18: 51
February 4— March 6	Yang Water	Tiger	Yin Fire	Snake	Feb	25	6: 34
March 6— April 5	Yin Water	Rabbit	Yin Fire	Snake	Mar	53	: 44
April 5— May 6	Yang Wood	Dragon	Yin Fire	Snake	April	24	5: 46
May 6 – June 6	Yin Wood	Snake	Yin Fire	Snake	May	54	23: 16
June 6— July 7	Yang Fire	Horse	Yin Fire	Snake	June	25	3: 32
July 7— August 8	Yin Fire	Sheep	Yin Fire	Snake	July	55	13: 48
August 8— September 8	Yang Earth	Monkey	Yin Fire	Snake	Aug	26	23: 30
September 8 – October 8	Yin Earth	Cock	Yin Fire	Snake	Sep	57	2: 16
October 8— November 7	Yang Metal	Dog	Yin Fire	Snake	Oct	27	17: 44
November 7— December 7	Yin Metal	Pig	Yin Fire	Snake	Nov	58	22: 46
December 7 – January 6	Yang Water	Rat	Yin Fire	Snake	Dec	28	13: 31

Branch	Pig	Rat	Ox	Tiger	Rabbit	Dragon	Snake	Horse	Sheep	Monkey	Cock	Dog
Main Element	Yang Water	Yin Water	Yin Earth	Yang Wood	Yin Wood	Yang Earth	Yang Fire	Yin Fire	Yin Earth	Yang Metal	Yin Metal	Yang Earth
Hidden Elements	Yang Wood		Yin Water	Yang Fire		Yin Wood	Yang Earth	Yin Earth	Yin Fire	Yang Earth		Yin Metal
			Yin Metal	Yang Earth		Yin Water	Yang Metal		Yin Wood	Yang Water		Yin Fire

1978

Find your Day Here	Month Stem	Branch	Year Stem	Branch	Day	Day	Time
January 6 – February 4	Yin Water	Ox	Yin Fire	Snake	Jan	59	: 43
February 4— March 6	Yang Wood	Tiger	Yang Earth	Horse	Feb	30	12: 27
March 6— April 5	Yin Wood	Rabbit	Yang Earth	Horse	Mar	58	6: 38
April 5— May 6	Yang Fire	Dragon	Yang Earth	Horse	April	29	11: 39
May 6 – June 6	Yin Fire	Snake	Yang Earth	Horse	May	59	5: 09
June 6— July 7	Yang Earth	Horse	Yang Earth	Horse	June	30	9:23
July 7— August 8	Yin Earth	Sheep	Yang Earth	Horse	July	60	19: 37
August 8— September 8	Yang Metal	Monkey	Yang Earth	Horse	Aug	31	5: 18
September 8 – October 9	Yin Metal	Cock	Yang Earth	Horse	Sep	2	8: 03
October 9— November 8	Yang Water	Dog	Yang Earth	Horse	Oct	32	23: 31
November 8— December 7	Yin Water	Pig	Yang Earth	Horse	Nov	3	2: 34
December 7 – January 6	Yang Wood	Rat	Yang Earth	Horse	Dec	33	19: 20

1979

Find your Day Here	Month Stem	Branch	Year Stem	Branch	Day	Day	Time
January 6 – February 4	Yin Wood	Ox	Yang Earth	Horse	Jan	4	6: 32
February 4— March 6	Yang Fire	Tiger	Yin Earth	Sheep	Feb	35	18: 13
March 6— April 5	Yin Fire	Rabbit	Yin Earth	Sheep	Mar	3	12: 20
April 5— May 6	Yang Earth	Dragon	Yin Earth	Sheep	April	34	17: 18
May 6 – June 6	Yin Earth	Snake	Yin Earth	Sheep	May	4	10: 47
June 6— July 8	Yang Metal	Horse	Yin Earth	Sheep	June	35	15: 05
July 8— August 8	Yin Metal	Sheep	Yin Earth	Sheep	July	5	1: 25
August 8— September 8	Yang Water	Monkey	Yin Earth	Sheep	Aug	36	11: 11
September 8 – October 9	Yin Water	Cock	Yin Earth	Sheep	Sep	7	14: 00
October 9— November 8	Yang Wood	Dog	Yin Earth	Sheep	Oct	37	5: 30
November 8— December 8	Yin Wood	Pig	Yin Earth	Sheep	Nov	8	8: 33
December 8 – January 6	Yang Fire	Rat	Yin Earth	Sheep	Dec	38	1: 18

Branch	Pig	Rat	Ox	Tiger	Rabbit	Dragon	Snake	Horse	Sheep	Monkey	Cock	Dog
Main Element	Yang Water	Yin Water	Yin Earth	Yang Wood	Yin Wood	Yang Earth	Yang Fire	Yin Fire	Yin Earth	Yang Metal	Yin Metal	Yang Earth
Hidden Elements	Yang Wood		Yin Water	Yang Fire		Yin Wood	Yang Earth	Yin Earth	Yin Fire	Yang Earth		Yin Metal
			Yin Metal	Yang Earth		Yin Water	Yang Metal		Yin Wood	Yang Water		Yin Fire

1980

	Month		Year				
Find yourDay Here	**Stem**	**Branch**	**Stem**	**Branch**	**Day**	**Day**	**Time**
January 6 – February 5	Yin Fire	Ox	Yin Earth	Sheep	Jan	9	12: 29
February 5 – 29,— March 5	Yang Earth	Tiger	Yang Metal	Monkey	Feb	40	: 10
March 5 – April 4	Yin Earth	Rabbit	Yang Metal	Monkey	Mar	9	18: 17
April 4 – May 5	Yang Metal	Dragon	Yang Metal	Monkey	April	40	23: 15
May 5 – June 5	Yin Metal	Snake	Yang Metal	Monkey	May	10	16: 45
June 5 – July 7	Yang Water	Horse	Yang Metal	Monkey	June	41	21: 04
July 7 – August 7	Yin Water	Sheep	Yang Metal	Monkey	July	11	7: 24
August 7– September 7	Yang Wood	Monkey	Yang Metal	Monkey	Aug	42	17: 09
September 7 – October 8	Yin Wood	Cock	Yang Metal	Monkey	Sep	13	19: 54
October 8 – November 7	Yang Fire	Dog	Yang Metal	Monkey	Oct	43	11: 19
November 7 – December 7	Yin Fire	Pig	Yang Metal	Monkey	Nov	14	14: 18
December 7 – January 5	Yang Earth	Rat	Yang Metal	Monkey	Dec	44	7: 02

1981

	Month		Year				
Find your Day Here	**Stem**	**Branch**	**Stem**	**Branch**	**Day**	**Day**	**Time**
January 5 – February 4	Yin Earth	Ox	Yang Metal	Monkey	Jan	15	18: 13
February 4— March 6	Yang Metal	Tiger	Yin Metal	Cock	Feb	46	5: 56
March 6— April 5	Yin Metal	Rabbit	Yin Metal	Cock	Mar	14	: 05
April 5— May 5	Yang Water	Dragon	Yin Metal	Cock	April	45	5: 05
May 5– June 6	Yin Water	Snake	Yin Metal	Cock	May	15	22: 35
June 6— July 7	Yang Wood	Horse	Yin Metal	Cock	June	46	2: 53
July 7— August 7	Yin Wood	Sheep	Yin Metal	Cock	July	16	13: 12
August 7— September 8	Yang Fire	Monkey	Yin Metal	Cock	Aug	47	22: 57
September 8 – October 8	Yin Fire	Cock	Yin Metal	Cock	Sep	18	1: 43
October 8— November 7	Yang Earth	Dog	Yin Metal	Cock	Oct	48	17: 10
November 7— December 7	Yin Earth	Pig	Yin Metal	Cock	Nov	19	20: 19
December 7 – January 6	Yang Metal	Rat	Yin Metal	Cock	Dec	49	12: 51

	Pig	Rat	Ox	Tiger	Rabbit	Dragon	Snake	Horse	Sheep	Monkey	Cock	Dog
Main Element	Yang Water	Yin Water	Yin Earth	Yang Wood	Yin Wood	Yang Earth	Yang Fire	Yin Fire	Yin Earth	Yang Metal	Yin Metal	Yang Earth
Hidden Elements	Yang Wood		Yin Water	Yang Fire		Yin Wood	Yang Earth	Yin Earth	Yin Fire	Yang Earth		Yin Metal
			Yin Metal	Yang Earth		Yin Water	Yang Metal		Yin Wood	Yang Water		Yin Fire

1982

	Month		Year				
Find your Day Here	Stem	Branch	Stem	Branch	Day	Day	Time
January 6 – February 4	Yin Metal	Ox	Yin Metal	Cock	Jan	20	: 03
February 4— March 6	Yang Water	Tiger	Yang Water	Dog	Feb	51	11: 46
March 6— April 5	Yin Water	Rabbit	Yang Water	Dog	Mar	19	5: 55
April 5— May 6	Yang Wood	Dragon	Yang Water	Dog	April	50	10: 53
May 6 – June 6	Yin Wood	Snake	Yang Water	Dog	May	20	4: 20
June 6— July 7	Yang Fire	Horse	Yang Water	Dog	June	51	8: 36
July 7— August 8	Yin Fire	Sheep	Yang Water	Dog	July	21	18: 55
August 8— September 8	Yang Earth	Monkey	Yang Water	Dog	Aug	52	4: 42
September 8 – October 8	Yin Earth	Cock	Yang Water	Dog	Sep	23	7: 32
October 8— November 8	Yang Metal	Dog	Yang Water	Dog	Oct	53	23: 02
November 8- December 7	Yin Metal	Pig	Yang Water	Dog	Nov	24	2: 04
December 7 – January 6	Yang Water	Rat	Yang Water	Dog	Dec	54	18: 48

1983

	Month		Year				
Find your Day Here	Stem	Branch	Stem	Branch	Day	Day	Time
January 6 – February 4	Yin Water	Ox	Yang Water	Dog	Jan	25	5: 59
February 4— March 6	Yang Wood	Tiger	Yin Water	Pig	Feb	56	17: 40
March 6— April 5	Yin Wood	Rabbit	Yin Water	Pig	Mar	24	11: 47
April 5— May 6	Yang Fire	Dragon	Yin Water	Pig	April	55	16: 45
May 6 – June 6	Yin Fire	Snake	Yin Water	Pig	May	25	10: 11
June 6— July 8	Yang Earth	Horse	Yin Water	Pig	June	56	14: 26
July 8— August 8	Yin Earth	Sheep	Yin Water	Pig	July	26	: 43
August 8— September 8	Yang Metal	Monkey	Yin Water	Pig	Aug	57	10: 30
September 8 – October 9	Yin Metal	Cock	Yin Water	Pig	Sep	28	13: 20
October 9— November 8	Yang Water	Dog	Yin Water	Pig	Oct	58	4: 51
November 8— December 8	Yin Water	Pig	Yin Water	Pig	Nov	29	7: 53
December 8 – January 6	Yang Wood	Rat	Yin Water	Pig	Dec	59	: 34

Branch	Pig	Rat	Ox	Tiger	Rabbit	Dragon	Snake	Horse	Sheep	Monkey	Cock	Dog
Main Element	Yang Water	Yin Water	Yin Earth	Yang Wood	Yin Wood	Yang Earth	Yang Fire	Yin Fire	Yin Earth	Yang Metal	Yin Metal	Yang Earth
Hidden Elements	Yang Wood		Yin Water	Yang Fire		Yin Wood	Yang Earth	Yin Earth	Yin Fire	Yang Earth		Yin Metal
			Yin Metal	Yang Earth		Yin Water	Yang Metal		Yin Wood	Yang Water		Yin Fire

1984

	Month		Year				
Find your Day Here	Stem	Branch	Stem	Branch	Day	Day	Time
January 6 – February 5	Yin Wood	Ox	Yin Water	Pig	Jan	30	11: 41
February 5— 29,—March 5	Yang Fire	Tiger	Yang Wood	Rat	Feb	1	11: 19
March 5 – April 4	Yin Fire	Rabbit	Yang Wood	Rat	Mar	30	17: 25
April 4 – May 5	Yang Earth	Dragon	Yang Wood	Rat	April	1	22: 22
May 5 – June 5	Yin Earth	Snake	Yang Wood	Rat	May	31	15: 51
June 5 – July 7	Yang Metal	Horse	Yang Wood	Rat	June	2	20: 09
July 7 – August 7	Yin Metal	Sheep	Yang Wood	Rat	July	32	6: 29
August 7– September 7	Yang Water	Monkey	Yang Wood	Rat	Aug	3	16: 18
September 7 – October 8	Yin Water	Cock	Yang Wood	Rat	Sep	34	19: 10
October 8 – November 7	Yang Wood	Dog	Yang Wood	Rat	Oct	4	10: 43
November 7 – December 7	Yin Wood	Pig	Yang Wood	Rat	Nov	35	13: 45
December 7 – January 5	Yang Fire	Rat	Yang Wood	Rat	Dec	5	6: 28

1985

	Month		Year				
Find your Day Here	Stem	Branch	Stem	Branch	Day	Day	Time
January 5 – February 4	Yin Fire	Ox	Yang Wood	Rat	Jan	36	17: 35
February 4— March 5	Yang Earth	Tiger	Yin Wood	Ox	Feb	7	5: 12
March 5— April 5	Yin Earth	Rabbit	Yin Wood	Ox	Mar	35	23: 16
April 5— May 5	Yang Metal	Dragon	Yin Wood	Ox	April	6	4: 14
May 5 – June 6	Yin Metal	Snake	Yin Wood	Ox	May	36	21: 43
June 6— July 7	Yang Water	Horse	Yin Wood	Ox	June	7	2: 00
July 7— August 7	Yin Water	Sheep	Yin Wood	Ox	July	37	12: 19
August 7— September 7	Yang Wood	Monkey	Yin Wood	Ox	Aug	8	22: 04
September 8 – October 8	Yin Wood	Cock	Yin Wood	Ox	Sep	39	: 53
October 8— November 7	Yang Fire	Dog	Yin Wood	Ox	Oct	9	16: 24
November 7— December 7	Yin Fire	Pig	Yin Wood	Ox	Nov	40	19: 29
December 7 – January 5	Yang Earth	Rat	Yin Wood	Ox	Dec	10	12: 16

	Pig	Rat	Ox	Tiger	Rabbit	Dragon	Snake	Horse	Sheep	Monkey	Cock	Dog
Main Element	Yang Water	Yin Water	Yin Earth	Yang Wood	Yin Wood	Yang Earth	Yang Fire	Yin Fire	Yin Earth	Yang Metal	Yin Metal	Yang Earth
Hidden Elements	Yang Wood		Yin Water	Yang Fire		Yin Wood	Yang Earth	Yin Earth	Yin Fire	Yang Earth		Yin Metal
			Yin Metal	Yang Earth		Yin Water	Yang Metal		Yin Wood	Yang Water		Yin Fire

1986

| | Month | | Year | | | | |
Find your Day Here	Stem	Branch	Stem	Branch	Day	Day	Time
January 5 – February 4	Yin Earth	Ox	Yin Wood	Ox	Jan	41	23: 29
February 4— March 6	Yang Metal	Tiger	Yang Fire	Tiger	Feb	12	11: 09
March 6— April 6	Yin Metal	Rabbit	Yang Fire	Tiger	Mar	40	5: 11
April 6— May 6	Yang Water	Dragon	Yang Fire	Tiger	April	11	10: 05
May 6– June 6	Yin Water	Snake	Yang Fire	Tiger	May	41	3: 30
June 6— July 7	Yang Wood	Horse	Yang Fire	Tiger	June	12	7: 44
July 7— August 8	Yin Wood	Sheep	Yang Fire	Tiger	July	42	18: 00
August 8— September 8	Yang Fire	Monkey	Yang Fire	Tiger	Aug	13	3: 52
September 8 – October 8	Yin Fire	Cock	Yang Fire	Tiger	Sep	44	6:34
October 8— November 8	Yang Earth	Dog	Yang Fire	Tiger	Oct	14	23: 08
November 8— December 7	Yin Earth	Pig	Yang Fire	Tiger	Nov	45	1:1 2
December 7 – January 6	Yang Metal	Rat	Yang Fire	Tiger	Dec	15	18: 02

1987

| | Month | | Year | | | | |
Find your Day Here	Stem	Branch	Stem	Branch	Day	Day	Time
January 6 – February 4	Yin Metal	Ox	Yang Fire	Tiger	Jan	46	5: 13
February 4— March 6	Yang Water	Tiger	Yin Fire	Rabbit	Feb	22	16: 52
March 6— April 5	Yin Water	Rabbit	Yin Fire	Rabbit	Mar	45	10: 55
April 5— May 6	Yang Wood	Dragon	Yin Fire	Rabbit	April	16	15: 44
May 6 – June 6	Yin Wood	Snake	Yin Fire	Rabbit	May	46	9: 07
June 6— July 8	Yang Fire	Horse	Yin Fire	Rabbit	June	17	13: 20
July 8— August 8	Yin Fire	Sheep	Yin Fire	Rabbit	July	47	23: 40
August 8— September 8	Yang Earth	Monkey	Yin Fire	Rabbit	Aug	18	9: 30
September 8 – October 9	Yin Earth	Cock	Yin Fire	Rabbit	Sep	49	13: 25
October 9— November 8	Yang Metal	Dog	Yin Fire	Rabbit	Oct	19	3: 59
November 8— December 8	Yin Metal	Pig	Yin Fire	Rabbit	Nov	50	7: 05
December 8 – January 6	Yang Water	Rat	Yin Fire	Rabbit	Dec	20	23: 51

Branch	Pig	Rat	Ox	Tiger	Rabbit	Dragon	Snake	Horse	Sheep	Monkey	Cock	Dog
Main Element	Yang Water	Yin Water	Yin Earth	Yang Wood	Yin Wood	Yang Earth	Yang Fire	Yin Fire	Yin Earth	Yang Metal	Yin Metal	Yang Earth
Hidden Elements	Yang Wood	Yin Water	Yang Fire			Yin Wood	Yang Earth	Yin Earth	Yin Fire	Yang Earth		Yin Metal
		Yin Metal	Yang Earth			Yin Water	Yang Metal		Yin Wood	Yang Water		Yin Fire

1988

Find your Day Here	Month Stem	Branch	Year Stem	Branch	Day	Day	Time
January 6 – February 4	Yin Water	Ox	Yin Fire	Rabbit	Jan	51	11: 04
February 4 – 29,— March 5	Yang Wood	Tiger	Yang Earth	Dragon	Feb	22	22: 43
March 5— April 4	Yin Wood	Rabbit	Yang Earth	Dragon	Mar	51	16: 46
April 4— May 5	Yang Fire	Dragon	Yang Earth	Dragon	April	22	21: 38
May 5 – June 5	Yin Fire	Snake	Yang Earth	Dragon	May	52	15: 02
June 5— July 7	Yang Earth	Horse	Yang Earth	Dragon	June	23	19: 13
July 7— August 7	Yin Earth	Sheep	Yang Earth	Dragon	July	53	5:33
August 7— September 7	Yang Metal	Monkey	Yang Earth	Dragon	Aug	24	15: 19
September 7 – October 8	Yin Metal	Cock	Yang Earth	Dragon	Sep	55	18: 11
October 8— November 7	Yang Water	Dog	Yang Earth	Dragon	Oct	25	9: 44
November 7— December 7	Yin Water	Pig	Yang Earth	Dragon	Nov	56	12: 48
December 7 – January 5	Yang Wood	Rat	Yang Earth	Dragon	Dec	26	5: 34

1989

Find your Day Here	Month Stem	Branch	Year Stem	Branch	Day	Day	Time
January 5 – February 4	Yin Wood	Ox	Yang Earth	Dragon	Jan	57	16:45
February 4— March 5	Yang Fire	Tiger	Yin Earth	Snake	Feb	28	4: 27
March 5— April 5	Yin Fire	Rabbit	Yin Earth	Snake	Mar	56	22: 34
April 5— May 5	Yang Earth	Dragon	Yin Earth	Snake	April	27	3: 30
May 5 – June 6	Yin Earth	Snake	Yin Earth	Snake	May	57	20:54
June 6— July 7	Yang Metal	Horse	Yin Earth	Snake	June	28	1:05
July 7— August 7	Yin Metal	Sheep	Yin Earth	Snake	July	58	11:20
August 7— September 8	Yang Water	Monkey	Yin Earth	Snake	Aug	29	21:05
September 8 – October 8	Yin Water	Cock	Yin Earth	Snake	Sep	60	23: 54
October 8— November 7	Yang Wood	Dog	Yin Earth	Snake	Oct	30	15:28
November 7— December 7	Yin Wood	Pig	Yin Earth	Snake	Nov	1	18: 34
December 7 – January 5	Yang Fire	Rat	Yin Earth	Snake	Dec	31	11: 21

Branch	Pig	Rat	Ox	Tiger	Rabbit	Dragon	Snake	Horse	Sheep	Monkey	Cock	Dog
Main Element	Yang Water	Yin Water	Yin Earth	Yang Wood	Yin Wood	Yang Earth	Yang Fire	Yin Fire	Yin Earth	Yang Metal	Yin Metal	Yang Earth
Hidden Elements	Yang Wood		Yin Water Yin Metal	Yang Fire Yang Earth		Yin Wood Yin Water	Yang Earth Yang Metal	Yin Earth	Yin Fire Yin Wood	Yang Earth Yang Water		Yin Metal Yin Fire

1990

	Month		Year				
Find your Day Here	Stem	Branch	Stem	Branch	Day	Day	Time
January 5 – February 4	Yin Fire	Ox	Yin Earth	Snake	Jan	2	22: 34
February 4— March 6	Yang Earth	Tiger	Yang Metal	Horse	Feb	33	10: 15
March 6— April 5	Yin Earth	Rabbit	Yang Metal	Horse	Mar	1	4: 21
April 5— May 6	Yang Metal	Dragon	Yang Metal	Horse	April	32	9: 14
May 6– June 6	Yin Metal	Snake	Yang Metal	Horse	May	2	2: 34
June 6— July 7	Yang Water	Horse	Yang Metal	Horse	June	33	6: 47
July 7— August 8	Yin Water	Sheep	Yang Metal	Horse	July	3	17: 00
August 8— September 8	Yang Wood	Monkey	Yang Metal	Horse	Aug	34	2: 46
September 8 – October 8	Yin Wood	Cock	Yang Metal	Horse	Sep	5	5: 38
October 8— November 8	Yang Fire	Dog	Yang Metal	Horse	Oct	35	21: 13
November 8— December 7	Yin Fire	Pig	Yang Metal	Horse	Nov	6	: 23
December 7 – January 6	Yang Earth	Rat	Yang Metal	Horse	Dec	36	17: 14

1991

	Month		Year				
Find your Day Here	Stem	Branch	Stem	Branch	Day	Day	Time
January 6 – February 4	Yin Earth	Ox	Yang Metal	Horse	Jan	7	4: 28
February 4— March 6	Yang Metal	Tiger	Yin Metal	Sheep	Feb	38	16: 08
March 6— April 5	Yin Metal	Rabbit	Yin Metal	Sheep	Mar	6	10: 13
April 5— May 6	Yang Water	Dragon	Yin Metal	Sheep	April	37	15: 04
May 6 – June 6	Yin Water	Snake	Yin Metal	Sheep	May	7	8: 27
June 6— July 7	Yang Wood	Horse	Yin Metal	Sheep	June	38	12: 37
July 7— August 8	Yin Wood	Sheep	Yin Metal	Sheep	July	8	22: 52
August 8— September 8	Yang Fire	Monkey	Yin Metal	Sheep	Aug	39	8: 36
September 8 – October 9	Yin Fire	Cock	Yin Metal	Sheep	Sep	10	11: 27
October 9— November 8	Yang Earth	Dog	Yin Metal	Sheep	Oct	4	3: 01
November 8- December 8	Yin Earth	Pig	Yin Metal	Sheep	Nov	11	6: 08
December 8 – January 9	Yang Metal	Rat	Yin Metal	Sheep	Dec	41	22: 56

Branch	Pig	Rat	Ox	Tiger	Rabbit	Dragon	Snake	Horse	Sheep	Monkey	Cock	Dog
Main Element	Yang Water	Yin Water	Yin Earth	Yang Wood	Yin Wood	Yang Earth	Yang Fire	Yin Fire	Yin Earth	Yang Metal	Yin Metal	Yang Earth
Hidden Elements	Yang Wood		Yin Water	Yang Fire		Yin Wood	Yang Earth	Yin Earth	Yin Fire	Yang Earth		Yin Metal
			Yin Metal	Yang Earth		Yin Water	Yang Metal		Yin Wood	Yang Water		Yin Fire

1992

	Month		Year		Day	Day	Time
Find your Day Here	**Stem**	**Branch**	**Stem**	**Branch**			
January 9– February 7	Yin Metal	Ox	Yin Metal	Sheep	Jan	12	10: 09
February 7 – 29,— March 7	Yang Water	Tiger	Yang Water	Monkey	Feb	43	21: 48
March 7— April 6	Yin Water	Rabbit	Yang Water	Monkey	Mar	12	15: 52
April 6— May 5	Yang Wood	Dragon	Yang Water	Monkey	April	43	20: 45
May 5 – June 6	Yin Wood	Snake	Yang Water	Monkey	May	13	14: 09
June 6— July 7	Yang Fire	Horse	Yang Water	Monkey	June	44	18: 24
July 7— August 7	Yin Fire	Sheep	Yang Water	Monkey	July	14	4: 40
August 7— September 7	Yang Earth	Monkey	Yang Water	Monkey	Aug	45	14: 28
September 7 – October 8	Yin Earth	Cock	Yang Water	Monkey	Sep	16	17: 19
October 8— November 7	Yang Metal	Dog	Yang Water	Monkey	Oct	46	8: 52
November 7— December 7	Yin Metal	Pig	Yang Water	Monkey	Nov	17	11: 57
December 7 – January 5	Yang Water	Rat	Yang Water	Monkey	Dec	47	4: 44

1993

	Month		Year		Day	Day	Time
Find your Day Here	**Stem**	**Branch**	**Stem**	**Branch**			
January 5 – February 4	Yin Water	Ox	Yang Water	Monkey	Jan	18	15: 57
February 4 —March 5	Yang Wood	Tiger	Yin Water	Cock	Feb	49	3: 38
March 5 – April 5	Yin Wood	Rabbit	Yin Water	Cock	Mar	17	21: 42
April 5 – May 5	Yang Fire	Dragon	Yin Water	Cock	April	48	2: 36
May 5 – June 6	Yin Fire	Snake	Yin Water	Cock	May	18	20: 02
June 6 – July 7	Yang Earth	Horse	Yin Water	Cock	June	49	: 15
July 7 – August 7	Yin Earth	Sheep	Yin Water	Cock	July	19	10: 31
August 7– September 7	Yang Metal	Monkey	Yin Water	Cock	Aug	50	20: 17
September 7 – October 8	Yin Metal	Cock	Yin Water	Cock	Sep	21	23: 07
October 8 – November 7	Yang Water	Dog	Yin Water	Cock	Oct	51	14:41
November 7 – December 8	Yin Water	Pig	Yin Water	Cock	Nov	22	17: 46
December 8 – January 5	Yang Wood	Rat	Yin Water	Cock	Dec	52	10: 33

Branch	Pig	Rat	Ox	Tiger	Rabbit	Dragon	Snake	Horse	Sheep	Monkey	Cock	Dog
Main Element	Yang Water	Yin Water	Yin Earth	Yang Wood	Yin Wood	Yang Earth	Yang Fire	Yin Fire	Yin Earth	Yang Metal	Yin Metal	Yang Earth
Hidden Elements	Yang Wood		Yin Water	Yang Fire		Yin Wood	Yang Earth	Yin Earth	Yin Fire	Yang Earth		Yin Metal
			Yin Metal	Yang Earth			Yin Water	Yang Metal		Yin Wood	Yang Water		Yin Fire

1994

| Find your Day Here | Month | | Year | | Day | Day | Time |
	Stem	Branch	Stem	Branch			
January 5 – February 4	Yin Wood	Ox	Yin Water	Cock	Jan	23	21:46
February 4— March 6	Yang Fire	Tiger	Yang Wood	Dog	Feb	54	9:31
March 6— April 5	Yin Fire	Rabbit	Yang Wood	Dog	Mar	22	3:37
April 5— May 6	Yang Earth	Dragon	Yang Wood	Dog	April	53	8:31
May 6—June 6	Yin Earth	Snake	Yang Wood	Dog	May	23	1:54
June 6— July 7	Yang Metal	Horse	Yang Wood	Dog	June	54	6:05
July 7— August 8	Yin Metal	Sheep	Yang Wood	Dog	July	24	16:19
August 8— September 7	Yang Water	Monkey	Yang Wood	Dog	Aug	55	2:05
September 8 – October 8	Yin Water	Cock	Yang Wood	Dog	Sep	26	4:55
October 8— November 7	Yang Wood	Dog	Yang Wood	Dog	Oct	56	20:30
November 7— December 7	Yin Wood	Pig	Yang Wood	Dog	Nov	27	23:36
December 7 – January 6	Yang Fire	Rat	Yang Wood	Dog	Dec	57	16:24

1995

| Find your Day Here | Month | | Year | | Day | Day | Time |
	Stem	Branch	Stem	Branch			
January 6 – February 4	Yin Fire	Ox	Yang Wood	Dog	Jan	28	3:34
February 4— March 6	Yang Earth	Tiger	Yin Wood	Pig	Feb	59	15:14
March 6— April 5	Yin Earth	Rabbit	Yin Wood	Pig	Mar	27	9:16
April 5— May 6	Yang Metal	Dragon	Yin Wood	Pig	April	58	14:09
May 6— June 6	Yin Metal	Snake	Yin Wood	Pig	May	28	7:31
June 6— July 7	Yang Water	Horse	Yin Wood	Pig	June	59	11:43
July 7— August 8	Yin Water	Sheep	Yin Wood	Pig	July	29	22:02
August 8— September 8	Yang Wood	Monkey	Yin Wood	Pig	Aug	60	7:53
September 8 – October 9	Yin Wood	Cock	Yin Wood	Pig	Sep	31	10:49
October 9— November 8	Yang Fire	Dog	Yin Wood	Pig	Oct	1	2:27
November 8— December 7	Yin Fire	Pig	Yin Wood	Pig	Nov	32	5:35
December 7 – January 6	Yang Earth	Rat	Yin Wood	Pig	Dec	2	22:22

Branch	Pig	Rat	Ox	Tiger	Rabbit	Dragon	Snake	Horse	Sheep	Monkey	Cock	Dog
Main Element	Yang Water	Yin Water	Yin Earth	Yang Wood	Yin Wood	Yang Earth	Yang Fire	Yin Fire	Yin Earth	Yang Metal	Yin Metal	Yang Earth
Hidden Elements	Yang Wood		Yin Water	Yang Fire		Yin Wood	Yang Earth	Yin Earth	Yin Fire	Yang Earth		Yin Metal
			Yin Metal	Yang Earth		Yin Water	Yang Metal		Yin Wood	Yang Water		Yin Fire

1996

	Month		Year				
Find your Day Here	Stem	Branch	Stem	Branch	Day	Day	Time
January 6 – February 4	Yin Earth	Ox	Yin Wood	Pig	Jan	33	9:31
February 4 – 29,— March 5	Yang Metal	Tiger	Yang Fire	Rat	Feb	4	21:08
March 5- April 4	Yin Metal	Rabbit	Yang Fire	Rat	Mar	33	15:10
April 4— May 5	Yang Water	Dragon	Yang Fire	Rat	April	4	20: 03
May 5 – June 5	Yin Water	Snake	Yang Fire	Rat	May	34	13:26
June 5— July 7	Yang Wood	Horse	Yang Fire	Rat	June	5	17: 41
July 7— August 7	Yin Wood	Sheep	Yang Fire	Rat	July	35	4:00
August 7— September 7	Yang Fire	Monkey	Yang Fire	Rat	Aug	6	13: 49
September 7 – October 8	Yin Fire	Cock	Yang Fire	Rat	Sep	37	16: 41
October 8— November 7	Yang Earth	Dog	Yang Fire	Rat	Oct	7	8:18
November 7— December 7	Yin Earth	Pig	Yang Fire	Rat	Nov	38	11:26
December 7 – January 5	Yang Metal	Rat	Yang Fire	Rat	Dec	8	4: 13

1997

	Month		Year				
Find your Day Here	Stem	Branch	Stem	Branch	Day	Day	Time
January 5 – February 4	Yin Metal	Ox	Yang Fire	Rat	Jan	39	15: 22
February 4 —March 5	Yang Water	Tiger	Yin Fire	Ox	Feb	10	3: 04
March 5 – April 5	Yin Water	Rabbit	Yin Fire	Ox	Mar	38	21: 14
April 5 – May 5	Yang Wood	Dragon	Yin Fire	Ox	April	9	2: 17
May 5 – June 7	Yin Wood	Snake	Yin Fire	Ox	May	39	19: 51
June 7 – July 7	Yang Fire	Horse	Yin Fire	Ox	June	10	: 13
July 7 – August 7	Yin Fire	Sheep	Yin Fire	Ox	July	40	10: 36
August 7– September 7	Yang Earth	Monkey	Yin Fire	Ox	Aug	11	20: 19
September 7 – October 8	Yin Earth	Cock	Yin Fire	Ox	Sep	42	23: 03
October 8 – November 7	Yang Metal	Dog	Yin Fire	Ox	Oct	12	14: 27
November 7 – December 7	Yin Metal	Pig	Yin Fire	Ox	Nov	43	17: 22
December 7 – January 5	Yang Water	Rat	Yin Fire	Ox	Dec	13	10: 02

Branch	Pig	Rat	Ox	Tiger	Rabbit	Dragon	Snake	Horse	Sheep	Monkey	Cock	Dog
Main Element	Yang Water	Yin Water	Yin Earth	Yang Wood	Yin Wood	Yang Earth	Yang Fire	Yang Fire	Yin Earth	Yang Metal	Yin Metal	Yang Earth
Hidden Elements	Yang Wood		Yin Water	Yang Fire		Yin Wood	Yang Earth	Yin Earth	Yin Fire	Yang Earth		Yin Metal
			Yin Metal	Yang Earth		Yin Water	Yang Metal		Yin Wood	Yang Water		Yin Fire

1998

Find your Day Here	Month		Year		Day	Day	Time
	Stem	Branch	Stem	Branch			
January 5 – February 4	Yin Water	Ox	Yin Fire	Ox	Jan	44	21: 11
February 4— March 6	Yang Wood	Tiger	Yang Earth	Tiger	Feb	15	8: 53
March 6— April 5	Yin Wood	Rabbit	Yang Earth	Tiger	Mar	43	3: 03
April 5— May 6	Yang Fire	Dragon	Yang Earth	Tiger	April	14	8: 06
May 6– June 6	Yin Fire	Snake	Yang Earth	Tiger	May	44	1: 40
June 6— July 7	Yang Earth	Horse	Yang Earth	Tiger	June	15	6: 02
July 7— August 8	Yin Earth	Sheep	Yang Earth	Tiger	July	45	16:25
August 8— September 8	Yang Metal	Monkey	Yang Earth	Tiger	Aug	16	2:08
September 8 – October 8	Yin Metal	Cock	Yang Earth	Tiger	Sep	47	4:52
October 8— November 7	Yang Water	Dog	Yang Earth	Tiger	Oct	17	20:16
November 7— December 7	Yin Water	Pig	Yang Earth	Tiger	Nov	48	23: 11
December 7 – January 6	Yang Wood	Rat	Yang Earth	Tiger	Dec	18	15: 51

1999

Find your Day Here	Month		Year		Day	Day	Time
	Stem	Branch	Stem	Branch			
January 6 – February 4	Yin Wood	Ox	Yang Earth	Tiger	Jan	49	3: 00
February 4— March 6	Yang Fire	Tiger	Yin Earth	Rabbit	Feb	20	14: 42
March 6 —April 5	Yin Fire	Rabbit	Yin Earth	Rabbit	Mar	48	8: 52
April 5— May 6	Yang Earth	Dragon	Yin Earth	Rabbit	April	19	13: 55
May 6 – June 6	Yin Earth	Snake	Yin Earth	Rabbit	May	49	7: 29
June 6— July 7	Yang Metal	Horse	Yin Earth	Rabbit	June	20	11: 51
July 7— August 8	Yin Metal	Sheep	Yin Earth	Rabbit	July	50	22: 14
August 8— September 8	Yang Water	Monkey	Yin Earth	Rabbit	Aug	21	7: 57
September 8 – October 9	Yin Water	Cock	Yin Earth	Rabbit	Sep	52	10: 41
October 9— November 7	Yang Wood	Dog	Yin Earth	Rabbit	Oct	22	2: 05
November 7— December 7	Yin Wood	Pig	Yin Earth	Rabbit	Nov	53	5: 01
December 7 – January 6	Yang Fire	Rat	Yin Earth	Rabbit	Dec	23	21: 14

Branch	Pig	Rat	Ox	Tiger	Rabbit	Dragon	Snake	Horse	Sheep	Monkey	Cock	Dog
Main Element	Yang Water	Yin Water	Yin Earth	Yang Wood	Yin Wood	Yang Earth	Yang Fire	Yin Fire	Yin Earth	Yang Metal	Yin Metal	Yang Earth
Hidden Elements	Yang Wood		Yin Water	Yang Fire		Yin Wood	Yang Earth	Yin Earth	Yin Fire	Yang Earth		Yin Metal
			Yin Metal	Yang Earth		Yin Water	Yang Metal		Yin Wood	Yang Water		Yin Fire

2000

Find your Day Here	Month Stem	Branch	Year Stem	Branch	Day	Day	Time
January 6 – February 4	Yin Fire	Ox	Yin Earth	Rabbit	Jan	54	8: 50
February 4 – 29,— March 5	Yang Earth	Tiger	Yang Metal	Dragon	Feb	25	20: 32
March 5— April 4	Yin Earth	Rabbit	Yang Metal	Dragon	Mar	54	14: 42
April 4— May 5	Yang Metal	Dragon	Yang Metal	Dragon	April	25	19: 45
May 5 – June 5	Yin Metal	Snake	Yang Metal	Dragon	May	55	13:19
June 5— July 7	Yang Water	Horse	Yang Metal	Dragon	June	26	17: 41
July 7— August 7	Yin Water	Sheep	Yang Metal	Dragon	July	56	4: 04
August 7— September 7	Yang Wood	Monkey	Yang Metal	Dragon	Aug	27	13: 36
September 7 – October 8	Yin Wood	Cock	Yang Metal	Dragon	Sep	58	14: 33
October 8— November 7	Yang Fire	Dog	Yang Metal	Dragon	Oct	28	7: 54
November 7— December 7	Yin Fire	Pig	Yang Metal	Dragon	Nov	59	10:49
December 7 – January 5	Yang Earth	Rat	Yang Metal	Dragon	Dec	29	3: 29

2001

Find your Day Here	Month Stem	Branch	Year Stem	Branch	Day	Day	Time
January 5 – February 4	Yin Earth	Ox	Yang Metal	Dragon	Jan	60	14:38
February 4 —March 5	Yang Metal	Tiger	Yin Metal	Snake	Feb	31	2: 20
March 5 – April 5	Yin Metal	Rabbit	Yin Metal	Snake	Mar	59	20: 30
April 5 – May 5	Yang Water	Dragon	Yin Metal	Snake	April	30	1: 33
May 5 – June 5	Yin Water	Snake	Yin Metal	Snake	May	60	19: 07
June 5 – July 7	Yang Wood	Horse	Yin Metal	Snake	June	31	23: 29
July 7 – August 7	Yin Wood	Sheep	Yin Metal	Snake	July	1	9: 52
August 7– September 7	Yang Fire	Monkey	Yin Metal	Snake	Aug	32	19: 34
September 7 – October 8	Yin Fire	Cock	Yin Metal	Snake	Sep	3	22: 18
October 8 – November 7	Yang Earth	Dog	Yin Metal	Snake	Oct	33	13: 42
November 7 – December 7	Yin Earth	Pig	Yin Metal	Snake	Nov	4	16: 37
December 7 – January 5	Yang Metal	Rat	Yin Metal	Snake	Dec	34	9: 17

Branch	Pig	Rat	Ox	Tiger	Rabbit	Dragon	Snake	Horse	Sheep	Monkey	Cock	Dog
Main Element	Yang Water	Yin Water	Yin Earth	Yang Wood	Yin Wood	Yang Earth	Yang Fire	Yin Fire	Yin Earth	Yang Metal	Yin Metal	Yang Earth
Hidden Elements	Yang Wood		Yin Water	Yang Fire		Yin Wood	Yang Earth	Yin Earth	Yin Fire	Yang Earth		Yin Metal
			Yin Metal	Yang Earth		Yin Water	Yang Metal		Yin Wood	Yang Water		Yin Fire

2002

Find your Day Here	Month Stem	Branch	Year Stem	Branch	Day	Day	Time
January 5 – February 4	Yin Metal	Ox	Yin Metal	Snake	Jan	5	20: 26
February 4— March 6	Yang Water	Tiger	Yang Water	Horse	Feb	36	8: 08
March 6— April 5	Yin Water	Rabbit	Yang Water	Horse	Mar	4	2: 18
April 5— May 6	Yang Wood	Dragon	Yang Water	Horse	April	35	7: 21
May 6– June 6	Yin Wood	Snake	Yang Water	Horse	May	5	: 55
June 6— July 7	Yang Fire	Horse	Yang Water	Horse	June	36	5: 17
July 7— August 8	Yin Fire	Sheep	Yang Water	Horse	July	6	15: 40
August 8— September 8	Yang Earth	Monkey	Yang Water	Horse	Aug	37	1: 23
September 8 – October 8	Yin Earth	Cock	Yang Water	Horse	Sep	8	4: 07
October 8— November 7	Yang Metal	Dog	Yang Water	Horse	Oct	38	19: 31
November 7— December 7	Yin Metal	Pig	Yang Water	Horse	Nov	9	22: 26
December 7 – January 6	Yang Water	Rat	Yang Water	Horse	Dec	39	15: 06

2003

Find your Day Here	Month Stem	Branch	Year Stem	Branch	Day	Day	Time
January 6 – February 4	Yin Water	Ox	Yang Water	Horse	Jan	10	2: 15
February 4— March 6	Yang Wood	Tiger	Yin Water	Sheep	Feb	41	13: 57
March 6— April 5	Yin Wood	Rabbit	Yin Water	Sheep	Mar	9	8: 07
April 5— May 6	Yang Fire	Dragon	Yin Water	Sheep	April	40	13: 10
May 6 – June 6	Yin Fire	Snake	Yin Water	Sheep	May	10	6: 44
June 6— July 7	Yang Earth	Horse	Yin Water	Sheep	June	41	11: 06
July 7— August 8	Yin Earth	Sheep	Yin Water	Sheep	July	11	21: 29
August 8— September 8	Yang Metal	Monkey	Yin Water	Sheep	Aug	42	7: 12
September 8 – October 9	Yin Metal	Cock	Yin Water	Sheep	Sep	13	9: 56
October 9— November 8	Yang Water	Dog	Yin Water	Sheep	Oct	43	1: 20
November 8— December 7	Yin Water	Pig	Yin Water	Sheep	Nov	14	4: 15
December 7 – January 6	Yang Wood	Rat	Yin Water	Sheep	Dec	44	20: 05

Branch	Pig	Rat	Ox	Tiger	Rabbit	Dragon	Snake	Horse	Sheep	Monkey	Cock	Dog
Main Element	Yang Water	Yin Water	Yin Earth	Yang Wood	Yin Wood	Yang Earth	Yang Fire	Yin Fire	Yin Earth	Yang Metal	Yin Metal	Yang Earth
Hidden Elements	Yang Wood		Yin Water	Yang Fire		Yin Wood	Yang Earth	Yin Earth	Yin Fire	Yang Earth		Yin Metal
			Yin Metal	Yang Earth		Yin Water	Yang Metal		Yin Wood	Yang Water		Yin Fire

2004

Find your Day Here	Month Stem	Branch	Year Stem	Branch	Day	Day	Time
January 6 – February 4	Yin Wood	Ox	Yin Water	Sheep	Jan	15	8: 04
February 4-29— March 5	Yang Fire	Tiger	Yang Wood	Monkey	Feb	46	19: 58
March 5— April 4	Yin Fire	Rabbit	Yang Wood	Monkey	Mar	15	13: 57
April 4— May 5	Yang Earth	Dragon	Yang Wood	Monkey	April	46	18: 45
May 5 – June 5	Yin Earth	Snake	Yang Wood	Monkey	May	16	12: 04
June 5— July 7	Yang Metal	Horse	Yang Wood	Monkey	June	47	16: 15
July 7— August 7	Yin Metal	Sheep	Yang Wood	Monkey	July	17	2: 33
August 7— September 7	Yang Water	Monkey	Yang Wood	Monkey	Aug	48	12: 21
September 7 – October 8	Yin Water	Cock	Yang Wood	Monkey	Sep	19	15: 14
October 8— November 7	Yang Wood	Dog	Yang Wood	Monkey	Oct	49	6: 51
November 7— December 7	Yin Wood	Pig	Yang Wood	Monkey	Nov	20	10: 00
December 7 – January 5	Yang Fire	Rat	Yang Wood	Monkey	Dec	50	2: 50

2005

Find your Day Here	Month Stem	Branch	Year Stem	Branch	Day	Day	Time
January 5 – February 4	Yin Fire	Ox	Yang Wood	Monkey	Jan	21	14: 11
February 4— March 5	Yang Earth	Tiger	Yin Wood	Cock	Feb	52	1: 45
March 5— April 5	Yin Earth	Rabbit	Yin Wood	Cock	Mar	20	19: 59
April 5— May 5	Yang Metal	Dragon	Yin Wood	Cock	April	51	: 36
May 5– June 5	Yin Metal	Snake	Yin Wood	Cock	May	21	17: 33
June 5— July 7	Yang Water	Horse	Yin Wood	Cock	June	52	22: 03
July 7— August 7	Yin Water	Sheep	Yin Wood	Cock	July	22	8: 18
August 7— September 7	Yang Wood	Monkey	Yin Wood	Cock	Aug	53	18: 05
September 7 – October 8	Yin Wood	Cock	Yin Wood	Cock	Sep	24	20: 58
October 8— November 7	Yang Fire	Dog	Yin Wood	Cock	Oct	54	12: 35
November 7— December 7	Yin Fire	Pig	Yin Wood	Cock	Nov	25	15: 44
December 7 – January 5	Yang Earth	Rat	Yin Wood	Cock	Dec	55	8: 34

Branch	Pig	Rat	Ox	Tiger	Rabbit	Dragon	Snake	Horse	Sheep	Monkey	Cock	Dog
Main Element	Yang Water	Yin Water	Yin Earth	Yang Wood	Yin Wood	Yang Earth	Yang Fire	Yin Fire	Yin Earth	Yang Metal	Yin Metal	Yang Earth
Hidden Elements	Yang Wood		Yin Water	Yang Fire		Yin Wood	Yang Earth	Yin Earth	Yin Fire	Yang Earth		Yin Metal
			Yin Metal	Yang Earth		Yin Water	Yang Metal		Yin Wood	Yang Water		Yin Fire

2006

Find your Day Here	Month Stem	Branch	Year Stem	Branch	Day	Day	Time
January 5 – February 4	Yin Earth	Ox	Yin Wood	Cock	Jan	26	19: 49
February 4— March 6	Yang Metal	Tiger	Yang Fire	Dog	Feb	57	7: 29
March 6— April 5	Yin Metal	Rabbit	Yang Fire	Dog	Mar	25	1: 30
April 5— May 5	Yang Water	Dragon	Yang Fire	Dog	April	56	6: 17
May 5– June 6	Yin Water	Snake	Yang Fire	Dog	May	26	23: 32
June 6— July 7	Yang Wood	Horse	Yang Fire	Dog	June	57	3: 38
July 7— August 8	Yin Wood	Sheep	Yang Fire	Dog	July	27	13: 53
August 8— September 8	Yang Fire	Monkey	Yang Fire	Dog	Aug	58	23: 42
September 8 – October 8	Yin Fire	Cock	Yang Fire	Dog	Sep	29	2: 40
October 8— November 7	Yang Earth	Dog	Yang Fire	Dog	Oct	59	18: 23
November 7— December 7	Yin Earth	Pig	Yang Fire	Dog	Nov	30	21: 36
December 7 – January 6	Yang Metal	Rat	Yang Fire	Dog	Dec	60	14: 28

2007

Find your Day Here	Month Stem	Branch	Year Stem	Branch	Day	Day	Time
January 5 – February 4	Yin Metal	Ox	Yang Fire	Dog	Jan	31	1: 42
February 4— March 6	Yang Water	Tiger	Yin Fire	Pig	Feb	2	13: 20
March 6— April 5	Yin Water	Rabbit	Yin Fire	Pig	Mar	30	7:19
April 5— May 5	Yang Wood	Dragon	Yin Fire	Pig	April	1	12: 06
May 5– June 6	Yin Wood	Snake	Yin Fire	Pig	May	31	5:21
June 6— July 7	Yang Fire	Horse	Yin Fire	Pig	June	2	9: 28
July 7— August 8	Yin Fire	Sheep	Yin Fire	Pig	July	32	19:43
August 8— September 8	Yang Earth	Monkey	Yin Fire	Pig	Aug	3	5: 33
September 8 – October 8	Yin Earth	Cock	Yin Fire	Pig	Sep	34	8: 31
October 8— November 7	Yang Metal	Dog	Yin Fire	Pig	Oct	4	: 13
November 7— December 7	Yin Metal	Pig	Yin Fire	Pig	Nov	35	3: 25
December 7 – January 6	Yang Water	Rat	Yin Fire	Pig	Dec	5	20: 16

Branch	Pig	Rat	Ox	Tiger	Rabbit	Dragon	Snake	Horse	Sheep	Monkey	Cock	Dog
Main Element	Yang Water	Yin Water	Yin Earth	Yang Wood	Yin Wood	Yang Earth	Yang Fire	Yin Fire	Yin Earth	Yang Metal	Yin Metal	Yang Earth
Hidden Elements	Yang Wood		Yin Water	Yang Fire		Yin Wood	Yang Earth	Yin Earth	Yin Fire	Yang Earth		Yin Metal
			Yin Metal	Yang Earth		Yin Water	Yang Metal		Yin Wood	Yang Water		Yin Fire

2008

	Month		Year				
Find your Day Here	Stem	Branch	Stem	Branch	Day	Day	Time
January 6 – February 4	Yin Water	Ox	Yin Fire	Pig	Jan	36	7: 26
February 4-29— March 5	Yang Wood	Tiger	Yang Earth	Rat	Feb	7	19: 02
March 5— April 4	Yin Wood	Rabbit	Yang Earth	Rat	Mar	36	13: 00
April 4— May 5	Yang Fire	Dragon	Yang Earth	Rat	April	7	17: 47
May 5 – June 5	Yin Fire	Snake	Yang Earth	Rat	May	37	11: 05
June 5— July 7	Yang Earth	Horse	Yang Earth	Rat	June	8	15: 13
July 7— August 7	Yin Earth	Sheep	Yang Earth	Rat	July	38	1:29
August 7— September 7	Yang Metal	Monkey	Yang Earth	Rat	Aug	9	11: 17
September 7 – October 8	Yin Metal	Cock	Yang Earth	Rat	Sep	40	14: 15
October 8— November 7	Yang Water	Dog	Yang Earth	Rat	Oct	10	6: 02
November 7— December 7	Yin Water	Pig	Yang Earth	Rat	Nov	41	9: 12
December 7 – January 5	Yang Wood	Rat	Yang Earth	Rat	Dec	11	1: 44

2009

	Month		Year				
Find your Day Here	Stem	Branch	Stem	Branch	Day	Day	Time
January 5 – February 6	Yin Wood	Ox	Yang Earth	Rat	Jan	42	13: 16
February 6— March 5	Yang Fire	Tiger	Yin Earth	Ox	Feb	13	:51
March 5— April 4	Yin Fire	Rabbit	Yin Earth	Ox	Mar	41	18: 49
April 4— May 5	Yang Earth	Dragon	Yin Earth	Ox	April	12	23: 35
May 5– June 5	Yin Earth	Snake	Yin Earth	Ox	May	42	16: 52
June 5— July 7	Yang Metal	Horse	Yin Earth	Ox	June	13	21: 00
July 7— August 8	Yin Metal	Sheep	Yin Earth	Ox	July	43	7: 15
August 8— September 7	Yang Water	Monkey	Yin Earth	Ox	Aug	14	17: 02
September 7 – October 8	Yin Water	Cock	Yin Earth	Ox	Sep	45	19: 59
October 8— November 7	Yang Wood	Dog	Yin Earth	Ox	Oct	15	11: 42
November 7— December 7	Yin Wood	Pig	Yin Earth	Ox	Nov	46	14: 58
December 7 – January 5	Yang Fire	Rat	Yin Earth	Ox	Dec	16	7: 54

Branch	Pig	Rat	Ox	Tiger	Rabbit	Dragon	Snake	Horse	Sheep	Monkey	Cock	Dog
Main Element	Yang Water	Yin Water	Yin Earth	Yang Wood	Yin Wood	Yang Earth	Yang Fire	Yin Fire	Yin Earth	Yang Metal	Yin Metal	Yang Earth
Hidden Elements	Yang Wood		Yin Water	Yang Fire		Yin Wood	Yang Earth	Yin Earth	Yin Fire	Yang Earth		Yin Metal
			Yin Metal	Yang Earth		Yin Water	Yang Metal		Yin Wood	Yang Water		Yin Fire

2010

Find your Day Here	Month Stem	Branch	Year Stem	Branch	Day	Day	Time
January 5 – February 4	Yin Fire	Ox	Yin Earth	Ox	Jan	47	19: 10
February 4— March 6	Yang Earth	Tiger	Yang Metal	Tiger	Feb	18	6: 49
March 6— April 5	Yin Earth	Rabbit	Yang Metal	Tiger	Mar	46	1: 48
April 5— May 5	Yang Metal	Dragon	Yang Metal	Tiger	April	17	5: 32
May 5– June 6	Yin Metal	Snake	Yang Metal	Tiger	May	47	22:45
June 6— July 7	Yang Water	Horse	Yang Metal	Tiger	June	18	2: 51
July 7— August 7	Yin Water	Sheep	Yang Metal	Tiger	July	48	13: 04
August 7— September 8	Yang Wood	Monkey	Yang Metal	Tiger	Aug	19	22: 50
September 8 – October 8	Yin Wood	Cock	Yang Metal	Tiger	Sep	50	1: 46
October 8— November 7	Yang Fire	Dog	Yang Metal	Tiger	Oct	20	17: 28
November 7— December 7	Yin Fire	Pig	Yang Metal	Tiger	Nov	51	20: 44
December 7 – January 6	Yang Earth	Rat	Yang Metal	Tiger	Dec	21	13: 40

Branch	Pig	Rat	Ox	Tiger	Rabbit	Dragon	Snake	Horse	Sheep	Monkey	Cock	Dog
Main Element	Yang Water	Yin Water	Yin Earth	Yang Wood	Yin Wood	Yang Earth	Yang Fire	Yin Fire	Yin Earth	Yang Metal	Yin Metal	Yang Earth
Hidden Elements	Yang Wood		Yin Water	Yang Fire		Yin Wood	Yang Earth	Yin Earth	Yin Fire	Yang Earth		Yin Metal
			Yin Metal	Yang Earth		Yin Water	Yang Metal		Yin Wood	Yang Water		Yin Fire

Four Pillars Chart

	Hour	Day	Month	Year
Stem Heavenly Influence				
Branch				
Main Element Hidden Element Hidden Element				

10 Year Luck Cycles

Age								
Stem Heavenly Influence								
Branch								
Main Element Hidden Element Hidden Element								

Recommended Readings

- Classical Five Element Chinese Astrology Made Easy by David Twicken
- Character and Health by Yves Requena
- Chinese Systems of Food Cures by Henry C. Lu
- The Tao of a Balanced Diet by Dr. Stephen T. Chang
- Healing with Whole Foods by Paul Pitchford
- A Manual of Acupuncture by Peter Deadman, Mazin Al-Khafaji and Kevin Baker
- Fundamentals of Chinese Acupuncture by Ellis, Wiseman and Boss
- The Foundations of Chinese Medicine by Giovanni Maciocia
- Classical Five Element Chinese Astrology Made Easy by David Twicken
- Flying Star Feng Shui Made Easy by David Twicken

Four Pillars and Oriental Medicine reveals for the first time the closely guarded secret of the connection between one's birthday and health. The Four Pillars or birth chart, which consists of the energetic influences of the Hour, Day, Month and Year of birth, contains an ancient esoteric code that provides the foundation for determining the constitutional health condition and how that condition is influenced throughout a lifetime. This book contains theories and techniques about one of the most closely guarded healing branches of Oriental Medicine.

Four Pillars and Oriental Medicine includes:

- An introduction to the principles of Asian philosophy; Yin-Yang, Heavenly Stems, Earthly Branches and Five Elements.

- The most user-friendly English translation of the Chinese Calendar.

- A step by step guide to calculating a Four Pillars birth chart and 10-Year Life Cycles.

- Learn to connect the Five Elements to the Internal Organs and calculate the condition of the Organs and Health.

- Identify major disharmonies of each Organ system.

- Learn to select Acupuncture points, Qi Gong practices, Meditation and Five Element Cosmology for balance and harmony.

- Evaluate Seasonal and Cycles of Time influences.

- Learn about Ling Gui Ba Fa Acupuncture—The Secrets of the Mysterious Turtle.

About the author

David Twicken, Ph.D., M.B.A., L.Ac., is a licensed Acupuncturist and Herbalist in California. He has studied Asian Arts for 25 years and teaches and practices Traditional Oriental Medicine, Feng Shui and Chinese Astrology. David as written "Flying Star" Feng Shui Made Easy and Classical Five Element Chinese Astrology Made Easy.